Like a Bird Flying Home

For John;
Jay did a wonderful job with
the writing and editing of this
book, and we are both very
grateful! Cheers,
Alison Clark

And it's a pleasure to tell
you this, since you know about
collaboration with Jay that
works out beautifully.
Here's to more shared trips,
Francelia

I hope you both enjoy this
John and Betty
with love,
Jay

WALTER CLARK

Like a Bird Flying Home

Poetry & Letters to His Daughter
from New Hampshire

———

EDITED BY

Francelia Mason Clark
& Alison Clark

Bauhan Publishing
Peterborough, New Hampshire
2013

The editors are grateful for permission to reprint selections published in *The Monadnock Ledger, Rivendell, Solo,* and *Views and Voices, Hancock, NH*

Sketches and watercolors by Francelia Mason Clark

Library of Congress Cataloging-in-Publication Data

Clark, Walter, 1931-2008.
[Works. Selections]
Like a bird flying home : poetry & letters to his daughter from New Hampshire / by Walter Clark ; edited by Francelia Mason Clark & Alison Clark.
    pages cm
Includes bibliographical references and index.
ISBN 978-0-87233-158-7 (alk. paper)
1. Clark, Walter, 1931-2008--Correspondence. I. Clark, Francelia Mason, 1938- II. Clark, Alison. III. Title.
PS3553.L294L55 2013
811'.54--dc23
[B]
                          2013004347

Book design by Kirsty Anderson
Typeset in ITC Galliard Pro
Cover design by Henry James
Manufactured by Thomson-Shore
Dexter, Michigan

BAUHAN PUBLISHING LLC
PO BOX 117 PETERBOROUGH NEW HAMPSHIRE 03458
603-567-4430
WWW.BAUHANPUBLISHING.COM

Moonlit May Night
(Eichendorff variant)

As if sky
Touched the earth
To splendor
It must dream back

And joy were a field
Whose dark woods
Muttered a brood of stars

And my heart
Wove itself over this place
Like a bird
Flying home.

Acknowledgments

Among the many people who have helped the editors bring this book to light, Jonathan Clark is foremost. Every warm exchange with him has not only generated the book but helped us to know its author even more profoundly.

We have been greatly encouraged and helped by John Ridland, who has kept and catalogued all of the letters Walter and he exchanged since 1953, by Howard Mansfield, Sy Montgomery, Jane Eklund, Steve Schuch, and Julia Older, readers with Walter for the community, then inspirations for us; and by David and Mary Alice Lowenthal, Parker Huber, David Robinson, Amy Markus, Cathleen Calmer and Roberta Beeson. Kitty Clark, Francelia's teammate, shot several of these photographs, as did Sally Allan. Sarah Bauhan, her staff and Jane Eklund have worked with us to make this book the best it can be. We have been cheered on by every NELP staff member who has heard about our project.

Finally, any errors are our own. Those we have found suggest there may be more.

Glossary for Shortened Names

Alan Howes, University of Michigan collaborator, co-director of NELP

Albert Dole, contractor and post-and-beam carpenter who built our house. He and his wife, Bonnie, live in Alstead and Lajas, Puerto Rico

Bob and Marilyn Mason, Francelia's brother and sister-in-law, from Melvin and Bozman, MD

George Randall, New Hampshire NELP teacher, musician, on Lake Winnipesaukee

Jim Clark, Walter's cousin, from Wolfeboro and Tuftonboro

Jonathan and Kitty Clark, Walter's brother and sister-in-law, from Wolfeboro and Boston

Pam Clark Reilly and Wayne Reilly, Walter's cousins, from Wolfeboro and Roanoke

Tim Benson, post-and-beam carpenter, from Springfield, Vt.

Hunt's Pond, on King's Highway, Hancock, the view from home

Lake Nubanusit, King's Highway, Hancock, location of Francelia's family's cabin

Lake Wentworth, Wolfeboro, location of Walter's family's summer home

NELP: University of Michigan New England Literature Program, taught in New Hampshire and Maine

304 Clark Street, Westfield, NJ, Walter's family's old homestead

Kineo, Rafie, Red Dog, Jefferson, and Fred, succession of family cats

Shush, Francelia's visiting horse from 2001 to 2006

CONTENTS

INTRODUCTION

Walter Clark said he drank from the well of the New Hampshire landscape. Everyone who knew him knew this. Not that Walter was talkative; he was a private person. But he was a poet, a teacher, and a continual writer. He accumulated friends, students, and co-workers over the course of his life who told others about his connections with the land.

By his teenage years, his friends had heard tell that he and his brother had rowed a very large abandoned herons' nest home to their summer place in Wolfeboro. In his career, University of Michigan students passed the word on the best educational field experience they could expect to have—Professor Walter's spring-term literature program on Lake Winnipesaukee. Finally, people in the town of Hancock learned that if Walter and others were sharing a poetry reading about the land, they wanted to be there. In these ways, a person who was private drew attention to what he cared about.

This book collects the poetry Walter wrote or revised during his fifteen-year retirement in New Hampshire, and the most descriptive passages of his "journal," his warmly detailed letters to our daughter, Alison. Together they show a sequence of moods and subjects. Only the poems reflect this sequence clearly, but they make a reader ask to know more. In context poetry and letters narrate a subtle development.

In the period of settling in to Hancock, "Time to observe such things," Walter celebrated his perceptions in letters of detail, surprise, and humor about living in this landscape more than in new poems. By the second group of years, he began an inward search in his poetry. Thoughts of what happens at death are the start of a striking progression of moods, moving from low to high to resolution. Beginning about 1999, he started a computer file titled "no date," which contained several poems trying to imagine death. His next file, from 2002, was handwritten, all poems exploring faith and prayer. Mention of a passing prayer is not rare in Walter's writing, but these poems are focused. This file lay on a shelf beside the computer, along with separate sheets of handwritten poems. The separate sheets of poems broadened in scope but clearly continued to appear when he resumed his computer file, and they persisted in being personal and different. By the last poems, both typed and handwritten, his thoughts of life's end seem no longer desolate but resolved, and humor has spilled over from his letters into the poems.

Walter's presence, and his letters to Alison, revealed almost none of this intense sequence. But his brother Jonathan's Biographical Notes show precedent. The son of a Roman Catholic mother and a Presbyterian father, Walter concluded his membership in the Catholic Church during graduate school. Lifelong he was strongly ethical, spiritual, and philosophical, but he never again accepted any formal religion. A struggle with spiritual boundaries seems almost inevitable, and his route through it can be followed.

Alison and I too made changes across these years. In 1995, she moved to Seattle for a decade, where we had happy visits with her once a year. Then, fortuitously, she returned to Boston, with the express purpose of being close to us. I taught locally part-time until 2000, then focused on becoming a watercolor landscape painter with Walter's full support. During Walter's inward period, sensing that he needed more private space than I did, I took up riding a trail horse.

As a whole, as well as reflecting philosophical changes, Walter's New Hampshire writings show his steady pattern of embracing a place. "It's always beautiful." Walter regularly said this of every season at the mountain pond that is the view from our Hancock home. But his entries suggest that the colder half of the year attracted him most of all. Though he had grown up in northern New England, now he had winter leisure for use of his energies. He sought outdoor time alone. Winter cold snaps, heavy snow, and walking on frozen lakes were challenges he welcomed. Ice-out or ice-in along the south-facing shore of a pond attract wildlife that was new to both of us and close at hand. March was a time when he wanted to wake up the landscape. October, however, the month of his birthday, seemed to elicit entries on striking beauty and subtle sadness.

"We never look back." Despite how often he said this, and despite the consistent joys evident in his letters, he did look back. Though he was a passionately committed teacher, he rarely had been a fully comfortable academic on a campus away from New England. Certain of his poems reflect this earlier, ambivalent mood. "The Prince" and "Messenger," even though he chose them for revision in retirement, are the most evident. "Gluck" reaches back to his student days for another kind of discomfort. Such feelings have a relationship to his life-changing successful enterprise in co-founding NELP, the University of Michigan New England Literature Program on a lake in New Hampshire. Classes were seminars; writing was in journals. Every member hiked and cooked or split firewood. Most students took up Walter's invitation to hike out on a "solo": to spend twenty-four hours alone in the woods with a tent and a journal. The program kept Walter visiting after he retired, and it continues today.

The last section of this collection, "Looking outward," reveals three smooth changes in proportion, all of them as a result of good news. First was Alison's return from Seattle to Boston. Renewed close contact naturally reduced (but did not finish!) the number of letters he wrote her. Second, in 2007 Walter successfully completed raising a large endowment for future directors of the NELP program. This effort reduced letter writing, but fulfilled him strongly.

Finally, a glance at the Contents pages will show that Walter wrote and revised progressively more poetry, culminating in work on at least eight poems in his last year. There is no doubt of his continued interest in publishing. He and his college friend John Ridland had refreshed their fifty-five-year-old friendship by agreeing to exchange critiques once more, with a first goal of sharing a poetry reading. This too was deeply fulfilling for him: he had worked his way through everything to return full focus on his body of poetry. In turn this returning flow of poetry documents his relation to the land.

— Francelia Mason Clark

One

Time To Observe Such Things

1994–1998

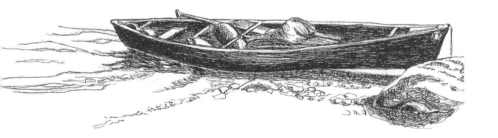

FRESHLY INTO HIS LONG-PLANNED RETIREMENT, Walter describes for Alison the new dimension in scenes she has known only from summer vacations in New Hampshire. She had never had the experience of walking at night between head-high snowbanks. He celebrates watching oaks bud from a high window, helping the carpenters build our timber-frame porch, canoeing among dragonflies in a swamp. This writing is one of his journals, but also very much a communication with her.

But it is still his journal. The paragraph about Wolfeboro in October introduces the characteristic counterpoint of places that Walter kept in his life. Now there were two places, two hours' drive apart, each on a New Hampshire shoreline—Hunt's Pond, Hancock, and Lake Wentworth, Wolfeboro—where he could go out and come back to a beautiful spot. He also kept a pattern of pushing north: he climbed Mount Washington, as he had done solo, with family, or leading NELP for years; in 1998, his favorite canoe trip on Moosehead Lake and beyond filled a journal. His letters to Alison, however, unless otherwise identified, are always from home in Hancock.

Alison was graduating from the University of Michigan. Her father's writing was aiming in part to help her remember her values and our loving support. In 1995, I was stocking our new home and teaching with Walter at NELP.

Walter's poem drafted in October 1994, "Walking Up the Hill," seems to generate from my absence as he walked up the hill, Tumbledown Dick, solo from Wolfeboro. He wrote "March on Figured Ground" with memory from his youth of a favorite month in northern New England. "Splitting Oak" came from clearing trees for our Hancock home. Gerard Manley Hopkins, so gently introduced to Alison, was a major figure in Walter's thinking, as a later letter will show.

He selected certain earlier poems to revise in New Hampshire: "Martian Anthropologists" is one of these. The poetry section sometimes includes passages of his short, reflective prose: "vantage point" is his screened Wolfeboro study; "I sometimes feel", part of an ongoing family history.

— F. M. C.

☙ It's always beautiful

March 1994

Dear Ali,

Last night I went for a walk after supper. The road to Nubanusit was completely dark and seemed to soak up light. On one side the snowbanks were about five feet high and on the other, seven. By contrast with the road, they glowed. I passed the contractor's house, lighted up like a cruise ship, and the older neighbors at the corner, where there were two or three lights but no sign of people. The next house on the right had light that leaked out on the far side, where I could see a head in a wreath of newspaper, and at the oldest house, only a faint nimbus around an upstairs room indicated that there was life in the house.

When I got to the landing, the wind in the tops of the pines made a lovely sound, and I could feel the "warm" (40-degree) wind sweeping up the lake against my cheek. The bob-houses of wise ice fishermen were huddled on the ice around the landing, waiting to be pulled off. The houses of foolish ice fishermen were still scattered around the lake, but hard to see in the dark. After these exhilarating sights, I came home and washed the dishes. Right now I am reading a book on ravens, and have ahead of me a new biography of Gerard Manley Hopkins, (a favorite poet when I was in college), Larry McMurtry's *Streets of Laredo* and an autobiography of the poet James Merrill, and also a trivial book on cats. More anon!

April 1994

For the past two and a half weeks I've been working with Albert and his crew on the new porch. When all is finished we'll not only be proof against blackflies, but also have cathedral windows in the bedroom. The porch will convert to a woodshed each September, making it much easier to feed the woodstove(s) through the winter. I thought you might like to see a journal entry [below].

7 April–Today I woke late. I was late for work! Cold cereal, hot coffee, toasted frozen bagel and I was into my Limmers and off to Albert's "Beamery." It was raining, had been all night, and snow was dying its death all around. I drove west on Route 123, the road getting steadily worse as I went along, up along Route 9 for a short bit (good road), then west through Stoddard and over Pitcher Mountain where someone has a herd of Scottish Highland cattle. Then through Marlow, now ennobled by PC Connection, a software company accepting telephone orders from all over the world. Marlow Country Store, however, retains its grunge, presided over by an elderly gent with specs who takes the entire day to read his newspaper. Then on to East Alstead, wholesome and unpretentious in the best New England tradition. This seven-mile stretch of road may be the worst in New Hampshire. Has frost heaves of epic proportions and a very bad complexion. I met a fellow the other day who had broken the front springs of his van on it. Just above an old water mill (in operation until five years ago), I turned north and spun down the narrow grooves of the road as if on a bobsled run. In a couple of miles I turned off onto mud roads impossible to describe, and reached Albert's.

May 1994

When I woke this morning I looked out the window (as easy as rolling over) and saw a plate of green vegetables—it seems that the leaves on an ambitious little yellow birch had come out during the night. The past couple of days have been full of things like this. Greenery is filling in the views around the house. Some of the trees in the upper story have put out leaves, but others, like the oaks, are holding their fire and have only thickened their buds. It's very nice to have time to observe such things.

The windows in our room are truly splendid. One can lie in bed and see up to the topmost twigs of the oak—the blossoms are just out and look like distant stars.

Down the Great Meadow with Bob and Marilyn. The day was hot and we raced a thunderstorm back along Nubanusit. Lots of dragonflies and three good-sized beaver dams. We stopped at a fourth that closed the mouth of a glen where the Tolman family had had a clothespin mill in the late 1800s. Conduits still carried water along the hillside, and the remains of at least two dams were plain to behold.

All the way down and back we were entertained by odd-looking dragonflies. They had two pairs of wings held vertically over the back when at rest, unlike any other dragonfly. Their bodies were of the green that Robin Hood's men wore and the wings were shimmering black. Some had a single tiny white spot at the tip. As fliers, they were somewhere between dragonflies and butterflies, but as WW I fighter pilots they were daring and inventive, particularly when engaged in the mating chase. At first we thought they were following us down the swamp, but then we realized that each stuck to its territory, passing us on to the next group below. They were a delight to watch for shape, color and movement. Marilyn looked them up when we got back and they turned out to be damsel flies. I would travel to see more.

The weather has been just grand. The trees are now at their height, red-tipped maples against the incoming brown-gold of the oaks, which are just beginning to change. Soon the highway will be afloat in falling leaves.

I spent this last weekend in Wolfeboro with the cats, who seemed to enjoy themselves. Visited George for supper [on Lake Winnipesaukee]. It was neat to ride back to Long Island standing up in his motorboat to look at the stars and the lights along the shore of Columbus Day visitors. He said that when he had returned the night before from a contra-dance there had not been a single light along the shore.

March on Figured Ground

Samples of night,
crows, patch
white land
scape, moon
light intrudes,
unblinking
wolves hear mouse heart
beat—first water
trill under snow.

Gerard [draft 4]

When you recognized a cross
you climbed up on it
and would consider the view:
it was hardly Pride's
fashionable oxidant,
the crux innate
of your dangerous calling,
affirming beauty
must sear, terror be ridden,
talent destroy,
beggar give all...
till the last Crumb
fall from the table.

Splitting Oak

Oak argues with you,
knots hidden in the fattest round.
Its grain eddies.

The woodsman pretends he is
a person from Olympus
parting two Greeks—
And he puts a hand
on each shoulder, etc.

Thoughts of the inner wood,
freed in a moment,
hesitate before moving
off on the shady breeze.
Oak is deep.
Oak is a muscular thinker.
Oak smells like vanilla.

Walking up the Hill Under a Full Moon

October leaves are falling.
On the hill across the valley
A gibbous moon is ghosting
Low and pallid

Five hundred moons have filled
Since I climbed this hill with you;
some fifty for slow pain
and a dozen for disdain
and many for forgetting

I feel my knee strings humming,
I hear my lung sack filling;
They set my mind to rocking
Each step is like a year

Each step that might have been
Like the colors of the fall
The walks I take
And the ones I can't take/

2

✍ Sitting in the rumble seat of NELP

February 1995

Dear Ali,

When the telegraph was first installed, linking Maine and Texas, someone excitedly told Thoreau, who asked, "Does Maine have anything to say to Texas?" If anyone should ask whether El Niño has anything to say to New Hampshire, the answer is "Lots." Our weather has been weird, and only this morning is there snow on the ground which promises to stay. Nubanusit is clear of ice and our own pond has patches of white set in a scuzz of ice. Ever since we arrived back in a shower of rain, things have been deteriorating into spring, and only now is winter starting to get a grip on itself.

I went out to the far end of the land along the Derby Road and cut wood today. Very satisfying until I came to take down a monster beech tree, which went off at a ninety degree angle from the bed I had selected for it and got hung up in some oak. Right now I do not see how I am going to get it down. I might just as well have hung out an enormous sign, INCOMPETENT WOODSMAN AT WORK HERE.

I drove up to Wolfeboro last week (and down to the camp as the road was open) and spent the night. Conditions turned out to be astonishingly benign. Your mom's sleeping bag kept me very cozy, though the thermometer read ten degrees in the morning. I had breakfast at Pop's Doughnuts which put a nice glaze on the situation.

St Patrick's Day, March 1995

A bit about your Irish ancestry, in case you should want to have the information on tap. Your Grandmother Ruth Marie O'Brien Clark, was born sometime between 1898 and 1900 in Milwaukee, Wisconsin. Being older than your Granddad, she never went into too much detail about her exact date of birth. Her father, James Smith O'Brien, was the youngest of about six children. He grew up on a farm in central Wisconsin and was the only one of his siblings to graduate from college. That must have put some distance between him and them, since we never had any contact or heard about his side of the family. Your grandmother remembers going to visit when she was quite young. Her grandfather had a red beard, and when he picked her up there was a smell she later identified as whiskey. Your grandmother was always suspicious of the "Smith" in his name, and worried that the family might have been tainted with English blood, but in reading up on Irish history I discovered that there was a famous Irish patriot named Smith O'Brien, and it is likely that that was the source of his name.

All I really have to pass on about James Smith O'Brien is a few anecdotes. He was bitten by a pig as a child while playing in the hay. Recovery was long, and apparently the time he spent at home with his mother, reading and hearing stories, was very important. Perhaps it is what marked him as one who would diverge from the country life. Later, one of his older sisters who had married and left the farm came back for a visit with her husband, who was a doctor. Young James was impressed and decided that he would try to become a doctor when he grew up. He attended the local normal school. I don't know whether he then taught school or not, but he did work his way through Rush Medical School (in Chicago, I think). How did he make his money? By selling books, among them sets of Shakespeare. Your grandmother reported that he knew Shakespeare well (more than I can say), so perhaps he memorized passages to use in his sales pitch. Even after medical school I think he must still have been a young country boy with no connections, no financial backing, no outside resources to help him get a start in the world. He settled on Milwaukee to start a practice, probably because it was an up-and-coming city, less competitive for young doctors than Chicago. The favorite family story, which you must have heard a hundred times, is about how he rented an office in downtown Milwaukee and waited for patients who never came. So after a while, he would take his black bag and go out briskly, walking in one direction or another as if on a house call (doctors made house calls in those days). He was athletic and liked to box, so he joined the athletic club and there he made some contacts.

Relatively soon he became the doctor for the athletic club and then for either the police or fire department. His practice grew. I imagine he worked VERY hard. He became affiliated with the Catholic Hospital in Milwaukee and eventually became its president. So there you have a variant on the Dick Whittington story ("Three times Lord Mayor of London") as, of course, many immigrant families do. This letter is already too long, but I will save it in a sort of family history I am working on.

May 1995

[Visiting NELP at Camp Kabeyun, Alton Bay, Lake Winnipesaukee] Everyone else here got up very early yesterday and headed off for Bar Harbor. I have the place to myself except for the occasional inquisitive convertible. Offshore, a flotilla of boats scourges the waves, shortly to be scourged themselves by the thunderstorm that will make this a brief letter. Outside my window, the beech leaves have not only come out within the past five days, but have also grown to full size, exhibiting the perfection of spring that the bugs will not allow to last long.

I'm enjoying sitting in the rumble seat of NELP. It's especially nice to know that if one of the vans crashes on the way to Maine, or the way back to Ann Arbor, I shall not have to be the one to write letters to parents. Nonetheless there is something about the nature of NELP that leads to a perpetual business among staff and I have not been able to dodge it. Last week we all piled into the vans and drove down to Robert Frost's first farm in Derry, New Hampshire, and somehow I found myself allotted the role of Commodore. No ships sank, all seem to have had a good time, and it was quite moving to walk through the sparsely furnished little house and tiny carriage barn and imagine what fine poetry got written there and what fine poetry later on harked back to the short span of years 1900–1909, during which four children were born to the Frosts and two died. I have a book which reprints the journals Frost encouraged his six-year-old daughter to start in those days, and which she kept through the end of their stay. It's neat.

This is a Class A NELP, both in terms of NELP and of staff. The cook, no more experienced than you at such things, is doing one of the best jobs ever. Two other new staff, one a former NELPer and one not, are doing fine. Your mother recited from African epic the other night and received much praise. Her drawing classes are very popular and so are her other classes.

The ostensible purpose of this letter is to thank you for the Gray book. [a gift of *Gray's Anatomy*]. I had heard the name of Asa Gray, but had not known before what exploits he was guilty of. My first official use of the book was to look up False Hellebore, which may be seen in the low-lying woods and swamps around the base of Mt. Chocorua, and looks like a visual of the kind of blast a Baroque trumpeter might blow. It will be helpful to me in reading in Thoreau, since he is not above identifying a plant by its Latin name and letting matters go at that.

The sky is darkening and the sound of motorboats is starting to fade, so I think I shall bring this to an end.

April 1997

Dear Ali,

An exciting time of year here. Last weekend we were up to our thighs in snow. Today is gray and rainy, temperature around forty, and the snow is all gone except where the trucks made piles, patches in the woods, and a long dark line of dirt-colored stuff on the north-facing side of country roads. It's now about 11 a.m. We slept in this morning. Then I made myself a messcupful of black French coffee and let the cats out (they departed slowly in line of seniority, like 18th-century British frigates departing harbor). Then I drove downtown for the *Sunday Times* and had a doughnut.

I had been planning to go up to Wolfeboro the last day of March, but the storm put me off, so I will do so later this week or early next. This is one of the nicest times of year to be there, though things can be mucky. I'll park my car at the top of the road and walk down. The ice will either be still in or just out, so I may get to be the first canoeist of the year. It's a good time to put some fertilizer where the day lilies, hydrangea and lilies of the valley will appear later on. Nice as Wolfeboro is with a crowd in residence, I like it in solitary mode too, when the water birds come much closer and you sit on the most accommodating front porch to watch the sunset.

We have bought a very fine (queen-sized) futon. It arrived yesterday and we promptly set it up on the porch in its bed mode, and used it last night. Amazing how much louder the outdoors is when you sleep on the porch. Frogs and toads were as loud as the Boston Pops. I heard the loud crack of a branch in the middle of the night—which might have been a deer, and the birds this morning were positively vulgar at 5 a.m. To top it all off, Kineo descended like a bomb from one of the overhead beams at an unknown hour of darkness.

August 1997

In the garden we now have about ten immense tomato plants which are getting ready to fire a broadside. We have had first fruits of six broccoli plants and have enjoyed watching the peas try to strangle the Brussels sprouts. Beets have provided some tasty greens as well as some shy little fruits. The exotic day lilies purchased from Tranquil Lake Nurseries have done well, except for a couple that have too much shade. There is a Freshman Peony, of which great things are hoped for in its Sophomore year, as well as some lilies of the valley planted by your mother along the back walk. We shall have to see how they survive the winter.

A couple of days ago your mother had a fine birthday surprise
for me. We put the canoe on top of the truck and off she drove,
with me in the passenger seat. I suggested that perhaps she might
want to blindfold me. She offered to stop and do so, but I said
I guessed that I preferred not to. We drove down to a swamp
east of town and put in at an unlikely-looking spot; but things
opened up and pretty soon it turned out that we were on the river that runs from Peterborough to Hillsborough. The land was
low and we could see late afternoon sunshine on mountains to
left and to right. There were hardly any houses or open pasture
lands to be seen. After a while we came to a dam. Your mother
opened her canoe bag and took out a tweed coat for me and a
dress for her. Then we walked about a quarter of a mile along
a railroad track until we came into the center of Bennington,
where it turned out that she had made a reservation for supper at
a lovely little restaurant. We ate until we could hardly move and
then tottered back along the tracks in the dusk. Fortunately there
was half a moon. It took us about an hour and a half to get back
to our starting point, but the night was clear and warm. It was a
lovely surprise—one I won't soon forget.

The day after tomorrow I get a chance to return the favor, as
a surprise 30th wedding anniversary celebration is in place. There
will be about 20+ guests—and after supper a contra-dance caller
and two musicians will arrive. George is coming down, plus rela-
tives on both sides and friends.

If you want to see the beavers on our pond you have to look for
them and for their houses, which merge with the land in nooks
and coves. As neighbors, they are not to be ignored, any more
than the human who helps himself to a peavey left by the wall at
the edge of the road. For several days, the spillway at our dam
had been accumulating sticks and branches, seemingly stranded
there by recent heavy rains. Last night when I walked down to

the pond to see a rare sunset, the low part of the path was awash and I had to turn back.

So this morning I took a spade and a hoe and walked down to the dam. Sure enough, the ten-foot spillway had been bridged and the pond waters were a good four inches above the lip. I lay down on the abutment and began to unbeaver this dam. Its structure was something like this: On top lay four or five good-sized poles, facing up and down stream and from four to ten feet long. They seemed like the most recent additions and appeared to hold everything else down. Underneath lay a chaotic mish-mash of twigs and bushes in which blueberries seemed to pre-dominate. I noticed quite a few twigs from which the bark had been delicately nibbled, as if to a beaver business and nutrition were a desirable combination. Underneath the textural matting lay another layer of long branches of various species. I removed these as much as I could so they wouldn't catch in the culvert that went under the road, but some swept down the spillway before I could reach them, or were swept by poor hoemanship. The bottom layer of thicker branches was cunningly lodged. Some ends stuck into the slots for the batter-boards (is this the right word?). Some were anchored in mud above the spillway, others wedged across the concrete abutments. Together they formed a sturdy buttress. As I got down and into this layer, the mortar of the thing, which was all on the upstream side, became more apparent. It consisted of long strings of pond weed at the base. From the look of them, the beaver may have dived down and yanked them from the bottom, roots and all. Mud had been plastered over these, and a surprising quantity of leaves, more than would have naturally floated there, I believe.

By this time, I had made openings on left and right sides, and the water was gushing through and boiling in the catch basin be-low. Taking a long pole, which the architect had left handy at the end of his night's work, I tried to poke loose the central island, which lurched once, then swept grandly down into the great boil of muddy water, broken sticks, and leaves swimming for their lives. It was a real satisfaction to succeed in this job, not that the beaver won't be back again tonight. My canoe experiences with beaver dams have filled me with respect for the thoroughness of their construction and for the sheer untidy bristliness of them which, like some personalities, warns a person off. It is the same satisfaction one feels in making a friend of someone who holds the rest of the world at arms length. I must not forget to mention the sheer pleasure of guiltless destruction.

What strikes me, thinking back about this beaver work, is the variety and complexity of behaviors that take place. It's not just that different kinds of wood are needed for the base construction, the textural mid-layer, or weight on top, but that time, place, and selection are involved, as well. The process has a symphonic quality. It's not stripped, like the tasks rats are "taught" to perform in mazes. The psychologist who wanted to teach rats to make dams would have his work cut out for him indeed. Not that the challenge won't be taken up sometime by a Worthy Rat Man. If we turn things upside down, the differences become more clear. The average rat can teach the average psychologist to perform the average maze task in a single repetition. This is because the student already knows what he is being taught and actually pretends to be teaching it. After deconstructing the beaver's maze, however, I find that I have merely glanced at the syllabus. Many mysteries remain for my instruction, but like the Old Man of the Sea, this teacher is a slippery fellow and will not soon be caught. It may be that I need to take a lab course, since construction itself has much to offer.

December 1997

We have had almost no snow for the better part of a month, which means that we have been able to watch the progression of pond freezing—which started out with the water part rolling around in the middle, coming nearer or going farther from the ice around the edges according to the direction of the wind. Then, all of a sudden it was frozen over with a thin black skim in the middle. [Warm days] would age it a bit, and the cold nights would freeze the bubbles in. Now we could walk across if we wanted to take the chance, but that can wait. In the meantime I can hear it behind me as I type this, rumbling and belching, stretching a tiny bit at a time in the sun of mid-morning. It tends to be quiet in the middle of the day and then starts up again around 4 p.m. as the temperature goes down. The other day your Mom and I were having our morning coffee and viewing it in an idle manner, when suddenly a small coyote, or more likely, large fox appeared trotting by on the ice. We feared for our edible cats, but the fox (?) just kept going.

Hylidae (peepers)

Spirits of warriors
shout from the banquet
their weird jubilation
across the abyss.
We thrill in ecstatic
(assent) to the pattern.

Haiku

Faraway firefly
Flashes, or is it a star?
An old love matter?

Martian Anthropologists

Once the way was prepared
In the popular press
They'd skipped in the back door
While we watched the TV.

They looked like—just us;
But with credible tact
Allowed us to see
Pulsing energy fields.

With what graceful address
They spoke words in our tongue!
We'd not met before
A people so foreign.

Yet knowing—hard to assess.
Were they brusque to a fault?
Did they speak in high gabble,
Never, never sit still?

These things all could see
And probably handle
Were it not for the thought
Of some Paradise Lost.

They just wanted our dreams
And some memories too,
Which they could record
Without causing us harm.

And they paid in cold cash,
And the money was good,
And some politicians
Shook each one by the hand.

In such manner and wise
They'd circled the Globe,
Astonishing all,
Pleasing more than a few.

When they all met once more
In Roswell, New Mex.
And before we quite knew
Had quitted this shore.

And what have they left?
A mirror, we hear
In darkest New Guinea
And a handful of objects
Whose use isn't quite clear.

[From drafted family history]

I sometimes feel as if my personality is inhabited by the camp of Clarks, WASPS to the hilt, and the camp of O'Briens: celtic, bitter, witty, devious, private, realistic in the way of a people who have always been poor, unforgiving, judgmental, empathic (to which Clarks are deaf), quick to take offense but slow to show it—I'm leaving a few adjectives out because I'm not sure what they should be—topping things off with "proud in the specially debilitating way of those whose manner of living is humble." That sounds a bit dramatic, and is. Haven't got it right, but there's something there.

[From joining a NELP writing]

My vantage point is a shack in the woods with a screened side opening on a small glade. It does not fill with fireflies more than once or twice a year. Normally a sighting is seldom enough to give rise to self-congratulation. The occasional little wanderer moves through in an assured manner. It is as if a tiny balloon were passing down the aisle of trees outside. Presumably an adventurer in a wicker basket slung beneath is eating roast chicken and throwing the bones negligently over the side. The balloon's canopy blinks from time to time like an old fashioned light bulb whose current is cut off at the very moment it is being turned on.

Didn't trust the church church! Squabbles between Cath. mom / Prot. Dad was sure abt god, but was enthusiastic abt praise + Prayer.

3

✖ Climbed Washington yesterday

May 1998

Dear Ali,

Climbed Washington yesterday from here, which meant getting up at 5 a.m. and being off by 5:30. Took the Jewel Trail,
which goes off to the north from the Cog Railway Base Station and comes in on the main trail from the north peaks just
to the south of Mt. Clay. I liked the lower sections of the trail
very much, but the going was quite stony in the upper part and
the ridge section took longer than I had anticipated despite a
strong wind at my back. Still, things went very well and I was
on the summit about 1 pm. Winds of 40 mph for the upper half
of the climb reached 70 during the last quarter mile. When it
got to be that strong I would stop in the gusts and try to get
a bit further in the lapses. This worked out all right, but I was
glad there was shelter ahead (complete with flying ice and a pattern of rime on the concrete posts of the summit station). The
place was jammed and it seemed as if another coachful of train
passengers pulled in every five minutes. It was a relief to be out
of the wind, which could be heard howling hungrily outside.
There were plenty of hikers, all looking as if a bit offset from
their normal selves. After a decent rest, I came down without
incident and was glad to re-enter the warm, sunny peace of a
late May afternoon. Had had to leave the cats locked in the
house and they seemed pleased to learn that I had not just
driven off and forgotten about them. After a brief infusion of
Bach I hit the hay (sleeping on the porch these days—which is
grand, what with peepers after dark and birds at 5 a.m.) I seem
to be not much the worse for wear today, but am taking things
easy on principle. Most of the garden is planted anyhow (*pace*
bugs), and I have to put together a new raised garden and fill
it with dirt before the tomatoes can be planted. Officially they

should go in the 5th of June, but I think we will take advantage of El Niño to put them in a few days early this year.

Your Mom and I drove over to Albert and Bonnie's this morning for a Lady Slipper viewing. There were about twenty other people there and the hosts had put a couple of tables on the lawn. Everyone brought something to eat. We stood around eating strawberry rhubarb pie and oyster stew for breakfast, and walked around admiring Bonnie's stunning garden. I went down to the vegetable garden and picked up a few hints that I can put to use. The people were interesting. The woman who brought the oyster stew had been a starving artist in Philadelphia, but had moved to Alstead to be with her parents, who had retired there. She and her husband moved into the barn, but her husband has a study in the house. We passed both barn and house on the way home and I can testify that the barn looked quite rural. Another man worked in Tedd Benson's beamery—which is just down the road from Albert's house. He told interesting stories about the work there and the morale—which is very high. When Tedd Benson started to revive timber framing, about twenty-plus years ago, the physical details were plain. All they had to do was to take a few barns apart. But there were no people living who had done the work, so they had in effect to reinvent the processes by which these barns (and our house) were built. It seems that everyone is involved in most aspects of the building. There is a big emphasis on quality as opposed to speed and lots of top-down and bottom-up communication. It came into my mind that the way they run the company is probably close to your ideal of community living. He said, for instance, that seven of eight of them had gone for an eighteen-mile bike ride after work and then had a pot-luck supper.

The weather HAS been good, though coldish. Strong winds from the northwest for the past five days—the kind that wend big waves up at Wolfeboro and leave a pollen mark on the beach.

I may take a little trip down to Lenox, Massachusetts—where I grew up—and look around. I've been there a couple of times with Francelia, and once with you, I think, but we were always on our way somewhere else and I didn't want to take up too much of the family time. If I go, I'll surely spend some time at the town library—which was a very important place for me; walk around the remnants of Lenox School; walk around town, visit a couple of churches that were of significance in my youth; drive over to the October Mountains; and visit Stockbridge, Lee and Pittsfield, to which we used to drive for shopping or adventure. I have no illusions about the places being the same, but it's a nice way to remember oneself. The changes will be interesting, too.

July 1998

Next Sunday we are going to make our annual canoe trip from Nubanusit down to Harrisville. It involves a couple of portages, but is quite interesting because a couple of miles go through an enormous swamp and the second portage goes past the (considerable) ruins of an old clothespin factory. Your Mom is working on a history of the lake for the Lake Nubanusit Association and has turned up stories about the old factory. Wherever the early folks found a good drop of water they tended to put in as many mills as they could fit so as to get the most out of the water. Even in the dry weather of late summer, when they might only be able to run the mills for a couple of hours a week, everyone would agree on the time and the water might be used three or four times as it came down to the next level.

August 1998

It's 8 am. I've just finished putting the canoe on the pickup and am about to drive off for a day on the Connecticut River with Tim Benson, who lives in Springfield, Vt. More when I get back...

I enclose a copy of the latest, and I hope final, version of the barbecue poem. I am particularly fond of the word "corbeled" for all it does to make the abstract "MAGNIFICENCE" concrete.

The Barbecue of the Virtues
(For Parker Huber)

MAGNIFICENCE his annual Barbecue
Declares, to which THE VIRTUES all aspire,
Each with such weight of Pomp and Retinue
As may do Honor to the Perfumed Fire.
First among equals, COURAGE leads the van
Of Greeks who shun both debit and excess;
Stern JUSTICE eyes askance the Christian Vein—
FAITH, LOVE, JOY, LONG-SUFFERING and
GENTLENESS.

But Hold! What knocker at the corbeled gate
Is this, his homespun coat unrecognized
By Paparazzi thoroughly apprised
Of all Opinion holds for Good and Great?
'Tis Henry Thoreau, come with candid gaze
To flip a slab of tofu on their grate.

Lately we have been besieged by mice. Rabbis in their temples are disputing how the entrance was made. Some say they marched in through the unlocked cat door while the Clarks were at Nubanusit. According to this theory, some Ajax held the vast weight upon his shoulders, whilst the other hundred or so hurried in to take the city. These latter first ripped a hole in the birdseed bag, then ravaged a forgotten box of instant potatoes. Those that had not eaten themselves into drunken euphoria next attacked a strongbox of rye crisp. All the rabbis agreed: mice were out of control. It is their means of entrance that has splintered discussion into various sects and schools and destroyed the great peace and petty bickering of rabbinical disputation. Might the mice have walked in through another door (carelessly left open by a male spouse)? Might the minions of mousedom have wriggled in along one or another of the water pipes which pass through concrete and exist to the end of watering flowers? A significant school points to the porch; under which rustlings and exhortations are heard at night—and in the walls of which infinitesimal rumblings (a bowling league?) have been heard.

Much is made of the firewood, which littered the yard for too long, and had been gathered up just before the first discernible—not to say unavoidable—indications of influx. The poor mice, so runs the argument of an enthusiastic eastern schul, had no choice but to shelter from rain and cats. In fact the ten thousand mice that now infest the house of Clark are but a mere relic of fertility, a mite for a mort; the vast majority having succumbed to predators both domestic and wild.

How generous the Clarks are, say some. They will be rewarded ten thousand fold. For nothing conduces to spiritual riches more than charity, and of all charities that which does not announce itself is the greatest. And the Clarks have not been announcing the plague of these vermin.

Prospects of spiritual gain to the contrary notwithstanding, the Clarks have not even welcomed these mice. It does not matter that the mice are polite and have tried to stay out of sight. They are not welcome, despite their many precautions, videlicet, they have not sullied the guest towels; they have not streaked across the living room floor on a bet (nor in it); they have not interpolated themselves, as it were, 'twixt the cup and the lip. Is it not sufficient that they have tactfully confined themselves: out of sight under the floor of the basement study; under the pallets which hold next winter's wood; and—as mentioned before—in the inner walls of the porch where they operate a small bowling league for purposes of health and recreation, beguiling the tedium of their necessarily dark life? Is it not enough?

It is not enough. Against these mice the Clarks have massed phalanxes of traps. Here first the…

(To be continued… —but probably not)

October 1998

Have we had rain this week. Pots and great pots of it. The rain gauge in the back yard has had indigestion. But there has been some surcease.

It was mercifully over this morning and had not yet washed all the leaves off the trees, so your mother and I woke to dark burnished beauty this morning, lit by a few flashes of sunlight, and presided over by the dark gray clouds of autumn. How glad I am that the weather wasn't like this on my canoe trip to Maine. I have finished a draft of my journal for that, which I am now going over while waiting for contributions and three poems from Sam Manhart. You surely will not be able to evade a copy when all is ready.

November 1998

I have been realizing that fall is a busier time (has more things that have to be done) than spring. The garden is pretty well ready for winter, but the wood is not all in yet and the time is getting short.

I was up at Wolfeboro earlier this week. The water was off and all had gone, but the weather was lovely and I was able to continue work on the wood behind Jim's as well as blazing the boundaries of the land we will have logged this winter. I had a quart of exceedingly orange paint with me, and since the forester showed me all the old blazes when we walked the land three weeks ago I was able to do a proper job. Tramping through deserted woods on a warm October day is pleasant. As I was thinking about this I tripped over a piece of barbed wire and involuntarily painted a good swatch of nature orange. Perhaps the logger will see it and smile this winter.

I have started another batch of rye bread. (My rye bread is really good by now. Unfortunately, I'm the only one who really has a taste for it.) Any bread I make now starts with a gooey mixture of flour, yeast and water. I leave this out in a big pot so as to catch any house yeast that may be floating by (there is always yeast of some sort in the air). I'll add more rye flour later today, as well as a little, very little, molasses, so as to keep the yeast happy. More flour at intervals—close enough to feed the brew, far enough apart so that I can keep the whole thing going for two or three days without adding more than 1/4 of my total flour budget. I'll probably add a chopped onion at some point fairly early on. This will make it smell rather vile, but is good for the bubbling mixture. A kind of burnt sugar goes into the final flour to make the bread look black. This is cheating, of course, but bakers don't tell.

When all is mixed, you knead for ten minutes or so, adding flour to help with the inherent stickiness of rye flour, then let it rise for an hour or so, beat it down, separate into four piles, shape and put into pans, let it rise for another hour, bake and taste. Good, eh?

Fifty Springs Are Little Room

The merganser takes his shape
From a punctuation mark
In an unknown language
And disappears under the waves.

He bobs up again
Where you almost expect him
Like a refrain
In a dead language.

All the little fishes are running
Now the Shadbush is in bloom.
The white blossoms take pink
From the setting sun.

Masked clouds will soon be silver
And you will hear the calls of loons
Say the rinse of wetter weather
Soaks the blossom of the moon.

[Journal entries from *Canoeing Maine*
Sam Manhart and Walter Clark, 1998]

Moosehead Lake
(9-13-98, 11 a.m.) Awoke two or three times during the night. Wind blowing hard. Up at 6:30. Wind very strong from the northeast. Big white caps. Lovely shafts of sunlight piercing clouds to the east. Mist rising from hills to meet low scud. Coffee and journey-bread for breakfast. We sit and talk in the warm sun to the lee of an enormous granite ledge while only a few steps away the blast rages.

Penobscot River
(9-15-98, 7 p.m.) I went early to my tent and considered the bugs, which would be camping with us from now on along rivers. On warm damp nights such as this they can be truly bothersome. Blackflies are not the issue so late in the year, and mosquitoes can usually be kept out of the tent. You watch them dancing hopefully along the netting, and imagine what the Alaskan Oil Reserve must feel like, if a reserve be sentient, as the oil companies petition Congress to open it up. It's no-see-ums that occupy mind and flesh, raising welts on ankles and wrists, and invective at the dinner table. They infiltrate the tent when you enter and their bite is like the touch of a lit cigarette. Sam claims to have luck with his lighter. Attracted to its flame the bugs immolate themselves. My tent (more of this later) is too small for such tricks. I had thought to distract them by inviting them to make guest entries in this journal, but the results are predictably crass.
    "Yum."
    "Great entrée."
    "Type A, Myrtle."
    "I feel a buzz coming on."

Good night.

Two

Thinking Inward

1999–2003

First, in a mood almost imperceptible in his letters, Walter's poetry keeps working with what it may mean to die. "Crinkling my sleep ear," 1998, had mused on death, but now, in the computer file "New Poems, no date," he focuses most poems on it. His question may be, according to notes and drafts of the poems, Can a person who has felt it necessary to reject a formal faith claim anything at the end of life?

The letters continued to cheer and support Alison, who now lived in Seattle. Yet between the lines some suggest a somber mood. As he describes the solitary fishermen in bob-houses, he borrows a facet of himself he so often speaks of: "the point of it is to get out...and come back." He ends this scene of isolation, "Ice-fishing as a passion is mighty cold and inward." Perhaps it is like fishing for faith through the ice. In his New Year's letter, 2001, he echoes his poetry as he writes of crossing a frozen lake alone. His red jacket in a swirling snowscape evokes the vanishing figure in the poem "Umbazooksus."

Meanwhile, his letters also show Walter continuing his fruitful life unabated—teaching Thoreau, making maple syrup, working again as an apprentice to his carpenter friends, celebrating the cats. By 2000 he is extending his cherished project of hiking the Appalachian Trail by segments. "Toads on the Trail" may be the funniest prose in this collection. But on the trail, his surprising inability to live up to the promise of his own strength and savvy likely increased his inward mood.

He does share with Alison how important Gerard Manley Hopkins is to him. He encloses Hopkins' poem on spiritual crisis, and his poem on Hopkins' crisis. But these are most understandable in the context of the poems that he was not sharing. In this period of Walter's life, Hopkins, who juxtaposed his spiritual dilemma with an intense love of the natural world, offered a kinship different from that of Frost and Thoreau. Aside, Walter wrote by hand: "There are no dead letters to God, Gerard."

Then, Walter's poetry of 2002 suggests transition. The typed file carries a revised memory, "Gluck." The new handwritten file carries "Faith" and "Triptych," composed together, and "Exhortation: To Prayer." These are committed, passionate poems. Most of the ongoing handwritten poems are personal, emotional, and direct, some in a speaking voice. By 2003 , both handwritten poems seem to work to a new level of conclusion. Walter mentioned to me that he had experimented with hand-writing poems and that some of them were working pretty well.

—F. M. C.

4

✌ Only the faint hiss of blown snow

January 1999

Dear Ali,

After ten days of near-zero weather, which tested the wood stoves (they were found wanting) and reduced the cats to guarded sniffs in the doorway each morning, we had snow modulating into sleet, then rain, followed by freeze. When I set out on a walk yesterday afternoon the sun was out, the temp in the twenties—a real invitation. The thermometer dropped so suddenly that our driveway is a mess and the road has a two inch topping of solid ice, waffled with tire tracks and sprinkled with sand. The walking was fairly good. As I puffed up the road I could see far into the woods. Now that the trees are bare the bones of the land are showing; bumps and hillocks where great pine trees overturned long ago, and lots and lots of boulders. No wonder that Civil War soldiers chose to move on to more fertile lands when the fighting was over. I saw no animal tracks; the freeze had taken care of that.

Not much traffic on the road, but when I got up to the landing at the big lake there were pickups and cars with trailers parked by the side of the road. Snowmobilers were out in force, but ice fishermen even more. They had been driving past the house for a couple of weeks to check on the ice. Now it was thick enough (six inches) to bear the weight of a car. When I looked out over the frozen lake I could see a dozen bob-houses scattered over the ice. The architectural model for your typical bob-house is a telephone booth. First you replace all but a tiny bit of the glass with plywood. Then you expand things a bit, but not with too much enthusiasm. A hole in the floor is necessary, so that you can drill through the ice. It should be about a foot across. This gives one a peephole into what Thoreau called "the quiet parlor of the fishes" (no TV). Heat is necessary, which can be (and frequently is) provided by the human body plus alcohol, or by the addition of a very small stove. The heat of the stove must not anneal the bottom of your phone booth to the ice. Otherwise you'll have to fish it from the waves next spring. Bob-houses rest on a couple of short beams, typically four by fours. These gradually sink into the ice; so once or twice a season the bob-house must be lifted and cross beams be laid across their tops. I believe that Antarctic housing faces similar challenges. One final step remains in the conversion of phone booth into Palace of Chill; removal of the phone itself. For a phone would defeat one of the essential purposes of ice fishing, namely the isolation, temporary but tempting, of the ice fisherman himself. It is a male pursuit, requiring the minimum of stir and hassle, and leading either to solitary contemplation or the assemblage of good fellows under lax and nebulous conditions. The point of it is to get out—to exit the nuclear family—and to go somewhere for the enjoyment of a society, architecture and space designed for and by men— and then to come back. The going out and coming back are equally enjoyable, but the enjoyments are of different sorts and not equally identified as such.

Looking across the ice, I could see many small stovepipes, seemingly formed out of #8 tin cans, crazily pointed in the direction of heaven. No two houses were the same, though all had arrived by way of pickup truck or else on very small trailers pulled by four wheels of drive, and so meeting similar constraints of size. There was a quorum within half a mile of the landing, but outriders were to be seen at distant points, stubbornly asserting their individuality and Yankee reticence.

When it comes to the roof, bob-houses can be divided into the stylish or slanted variety, with implications as to measurement, fancy carpentry and heedless expense, as opposed to plain style, a flat sheet of 4' X 8' plywood clapped on like an old hat, icicles to form where they will. From these structures, accompanied by deoxygenated fishermen, emerge occasional lake trout, more [rarely] "landlocked salmon," as well as the odd pickerel.

But fish are few and far between. You could stand for a couple of hours in the middle of the lake, hearing for jubilation only the faint hiss of blown snow, generating your own excitement and not seeing a soul except for a solitary figure visiting satellite holes to skim the ice. Ice-fishing as a passion is mighty cold and inward.

Well, that's the news from Lake Woebegone for now. We have good memories of your visit here. Your mom claims that the cats were down after you left. It could well be, but could also be that the weather is not to their taste. You'll have to come in good weather sometime so we can put the theory to the test.

[On teaching Thoreau]

[Guest at University of Michigan writing program, Biology Station, Pellston, Michigan, Fall 1994]

challenge class to respond to interest & heart

November 1994
We're reading Thoreau's *Walden* now in class. There has been some resistance because earlier reading was easier, more contemporary and "had more plot." The day before yesterday was really a bad session. Students sat like bumps on logs, saying nothing. So I ended class early and said that the afternoon class was only for those who wanted to be there. Three people stayed away, but the rest made a real effort and class went fairly well. Right now I am feeling quite cheerful because this morning's class was first rate. People had done the reading, thought about it, and had things to say. I'm sure that moods—like weather patterns—pass over a group like this and affect our contact with the work we are doing.

February 1999
This is now the second year that NELP has had an email address for all new students. They have been back-and-forthing with considerable enthusiasm for the upcoming program, and also getting together acting, singing and other music-making groups.

I rather gingerly put a Thoreau journal entry on the line. A couple of staff members and several students responded with their own selections, and one girl rather unwisely asked whether anyone could suggest books to read. I thought you might be willing to look at my response. Part of the reason for all this foo-farraw is that in the past, students often found Thoreau too rough-edged. The attempt here is to make him more human. He seems to have been particularly good with children and tough on stuffed shirts.

A book that is fun, *Thoreau As Seen by his Contemporaries*, edited by Walter Harding and published by Dover Publications, is full of spicy gossip. Examples?

"You know my father worked for Henry's father when he was in the pencil business. Father helped to furnish the graphite. I tell ye, that fellow Henry was a lazy lad, and it was well he could write an essay on economy as they say he did—many a piece of pie he ate from my pail." Pat Flannery

"The children hailed his coming with delight. It was better than any fairy tale to listen to his stories of the woods or the river. To hear him talk they would gather around still as mice. What marvelous ways the birds and squirrels had which no one else had discovered. Who but Mr. Thoreau could tame the fishes in the pond, feed the little mice from his fingers, keep up a whistling fire of conversation with the birds til they alighted on his head and shoulders, wondering what friend could be so very familiar with bird language. Who else received calls from the moles—and how the children's eyes would brighten as he told them of the tamed partridge so proud of her family that she brought them all to show him and how in return for her kindness he shared his breakfast with the brood." Mary Hosmer Brown

"Lovejoy, the preacher, came to Concord, and hoped Henry Thoreau would go to hear him. 'I have got a sermon to purpose for him.' 'No,' the aunts said, 'we are afraid not.' Then he wished to be introduced to him at the house. So he was confronted. Then he put his hand from behind on Henry, tapping his back, and said, 'Here's the chap who camped in the woods.'

Henry looked round, and said, 'And here's the chap who camps in the pulpit.' Lovejoy looked disconcerted, and said no more."
Emerson

March 3 1999

We've only been collecting sap for two days but already have nearly ten gallons. That should come to between one and two quarts of syrup if we can make the evaporator work right.

March 30, 1999.

It's warm and sunny today. The big cats are luxuriating in the back yard and young Jefferson is sleepier than usual (a good thing) because of the heat. I pulled my taps yesterday, but we still have a 30 gallon garbage can full of sap in the garage, and there are a couple of gallons of half-boiled sap in the refrigerator. So tomorrow I will put time in at the outdoor stove and throw away what remains unfinished at the end of the day.

June 1999

The frame we are cutting is not very special for size, but it is of post and beam construction. We work with more than a hundred pieces of milled pine. The pine is green, that is, still quite wet, and heavy. I can just manage to carry my end of the longer heavier pieces. From long experience, Tim knows all the little tricks to avoid having to lift them any more than necessary. The whole set of logs is a kind of giant erector set, the pattern for which exists in Tim's mind and in rough diagrams drawn on draftsman's paper. "Cutting a frame" means cutting out holes ("mortises"), and shaping the ends of other logs to fit into them. The shaped pieces that fit into the mortises are called "tenons." In some cases holes are drilled through both the inserted tenon and its mortise, and an inch-thick oak peg driven through to hold the two in place. This is why you sometimes hear post-and-beam construction called "timber peg" construction.

Tim must not only hold all these pieces in his mind, but also their orientations and connections. An uncut twelve-foot pine timber has six possible orientations, corresponding to its four sides and two ends, but once it has been cut it has a single address in the completed structure which Tim marks in cabalistic pencil on its side. How does he keep all this in mind? I think when he is doing a timber frame he must be constantly going over the design in his mind—knitting the frame together again and again, now with reference to this timber, now that. He swims in a kind of sea of action and choice. Things are upon him and he must be ready because time is money and he has an assistant to keep busy.

Have you ever watched carpenters at work? They move slowly, with an unconsciously exaggerated step. I know now that the slowness and air of abstraction are probably because the person is thinking something like "one and three quarters, "left not right" or "the angle is 35 degrees on the inside." The carpenter's gait is partly because of the peculiar aspect of high mental effort—no one would walk through a library this way. It's also because of all the tools, pieces of wood and thick electric cord that are lying around. One walks prepared to almost trip over something, or to find a fellow suddenly backing out into one's path with a buzzing electric handsaw. Carpenters on the job have a peculiar consciousness of what is around and within them that is not like anybody else's. Tim has this consciousness. You can see it in his movements. He measures things twice and calls Albert to check before he operates on the patient. Albert calls him "the doctor."

Albert and Tim are interesting to work with. Tim has a questioning mind, as does Albert, so the fur flies when we are on break.

My jobs are the simplest ones. I'm particularly good at cleaning out the pockets that Tim has roughed out with his router. I go at these with wood chisel and mallet. Since the whole point of timber frame construction is to see the frame from the inside of the house, it really should be thought of as a kind of wood sculpture. This means that all the parts that can be seen should be done to a nicety. What my chisel does *inside* a pocket doesn't matter as long as there is room for the tenon that will be coming in. But the line of the outer edge matters a great deal, and I spend a lot of time making it perfectly straight.

Dear Ali,

We are having a burst of Seattle weather. It's cloudy and fog and rain are forecast. The pond, which had been booming and crackling, has been struck silent and there are puddles of water as glossy as mercury, standing here and there. When the inevitable cold snap comes it will be Zamboni-smooth and I shall be regretting that I no longer skate. There was a man in the Eisenhower administration named Sherman Adams who came from New Hampshire, and I can remember Time Magazine writing that he used to put Mozart on a loud speaker and skate to it in the morning. One could do worse, although of course it would be a form of noise pollution and an insult to the neighborhood dogs.

65fc! This, except for the exclamation point, is a greeting from Jefferson, who is sleepily, or cryptically, licking his paws on the desk in front of me. And now he's gazing with bleary good will at the keyboard itself—wondering if perhaps there is some small edible insect buried within. But now sleep overcomes him. He flexes the toes of one hind leg (cats can do such things), puts his head down and appears to go to sleep. But any new noise will wake him, or even the thought of something new in the edibility line. Perhaps that is how cats customarily wake up. It's snowing out and the interesting things in the world have all gone to ground and are sleeping. The cat's ability to sleep, or to inhabit some intermediate ground between sleeping and waking where the dreams are soothing and now and then a spot of philosophy gets done: this is an ability for humans to envy, since most of them don't learn or relearn to do it until they have lived a long time.

So much for cats. This one is stretched out on my green desk to his full yard and seems quite content/resigned. I expect the two concepts often merge in the cat world.

The weather has been grand lately, temps in the '20s at night and sometimes up to sixty during the day, mostly sunny. Today has decided to make up for all the good weather and there is a fine snow falling. It's covering all the bare spots and disappearing in the little slice of open water along the ice on the pond in front of the house. I've learned to look for ducks and perhaps even a heron there just as soon as the water is ten feet or so from ice to shore, and maybe a hundred feet along the shore itself. But nothing has turned up so far this year and I was beginning to wonder until this snow appeared. The birds know something I don't. Jefferson just jumped up to sit on the green table while I dash this off. He has had a strenuous few days lately. In addition to his normal attempts to tip Kineo upside down (which she takes more or less in good kind), he has broken the umbrella stand in the hall that came from 304 Clark St. in Westfield because he wanted to get at the Kitty-tease which it contained. Best of all, however, was his encounter with Lucy, the awkward but well intentioned lab who lives across the street and seems not to get as much affection as she would like. She approached barking, as is her wont, the day before yesterday. Jefferson has learned from the other cats to face her with back erect and eyes firmly fixed. This he did. Lucy made overtures, turning to one side while looking at him, and eventually lying on her back in the new-fallen snow and wriggling and grunting in a most undignified manner. Jefferson was unimpressed. Then he moved a few feet out from his spot in the doorway. Lucy wagged her tail and faced him. He arched his back and sidled in her direction. She moved off up the driveway about fifteen feet and lay down in a conciliatory manner while looking at the garage. Stepping high and slow, Jefferson advanced still further, his back arched and tail rigid. He was definitely radiating ill-will. Your mother and I, meanwhile, were watching the whole adventure with great amusement. Jefferson continued to advance. When he got within striking range, Lucy shambled to her feet and moved off up the driveway. The whole thing repeated itself four or five times. The last I saw, Lucy was disappearing into the street. So I whistled for Jefferson and he trotted down the driveway, very pleased with himself. One could almost see him dusting his paws off on his metaphorical trousers.

He got a lot of praise down here, along with admonitions not to overdo it. Naturally, I would like nothing better than to see him rout the Wolfeboro dogs in the summer.

September 2000

After we left you to the delights of Keene we rode on to where NY Route 55 crosses the Appalachian Trail and your Mom let me off around two in the afternoon. I must admit to the misgivings one has when starting an adventure of some magnitude. But the afternoon went well. I had only about 4 1/2 miles to hike and arrived in good time at a shelter with a beautiful view. The next day went well, too (7 miles), though I was pretty well tired out by the end of the day, and more than ready to lie down and feed the mosquitoes which had been following in my wake all day long. After I had been there a couple of hours two hikers arrived who had started in Georgia last spring. Their names (trail names) were "Strolling," a thin 6'9" with scientific interests, and "Chief," red-headed and interested in ecology. I gathered from their conversation and also their exclamations over the names in the shelter register of those who had preceded them that they were among the tail end of this year's end-to-enders. They were very pleasant to talk to and made much of not hurrying, but stopping to enjoy the views or whatever diversions presented themselves.

I left before they did the next day, having 12 miles to do before reaching the next shelter, and this is in fact what did me in as it turned out that the twelve miles included four peaks—each of which had to be laboriously climbed. Descents, also, were not always as easy as one would have liked. When I reached the end of things I was bushed and decided to spend the night at a bed and breakfast in Kent [Connecticut]. There I realized that I was ill-equipped for my hike. More important, I had set much too ambitious a route and would have to radically revise my plans, spending many nights in a tent at camp grounds, as opposed to pushing for shelters. This meant I needed a tent, but I had

[45]

thought I could get by without one. So I decided to abort my four-week trip; called your Mom the next morning and arranged for her to meet me up the trail the following noon.

Getting Older

Young ones imagine me
As they would not have themselves.
Young men warn the girls
Of what will be gone when birds
End feeding from their hands

I see these things in my mirror.
I have done with them.
It is well.
I am past caring for others' esteem,
But I had not expected this windfall,
Of thought's vast landscape
Bare in its dry polished beauty
To which I do not belong,
Though I may enter,
Traverse its _____,
Hearing the low whisper
Of the thin desert wind.

Ill-prepared to meet bliss,
the heart sets forth
upon that woeful journey
always toward home
it had not hoped to reach.

Thinking About Death

There is something in each of us
that has always been there,
but do not be frightened,
it is like a pocket of ore,
drawing us to it
through all the gardens;
and when we arrive there
in a hovering instant,
the shivering senses
our needle's nesting...

It Is Harder

It is harder to believe in oneself
than in Gods,
which is why there are gods,
who merit our praise,

myself being only a piece of glass
bottle at the edge of the sea,
turning and rasping
against the grain of days—

dry grain, scant life,
with only the hauteur of time
for relief,
and beauty's rotunda.

Time then, beauty,
traces of portent,
are something to reeve
from a gaunt searscape,

and we allow
every bottle
to carry its own message,
chancel its own Genie.

5

❧ I could barely see my home shore

January 2001

Dear Ali,

Happy New Year!

Suddenly the snow arrived after temporizing for a month or so during which we had lots of cold weather, but little cold stuff. It came on in late morning the other day as I walked up to the end of the King's Highway and then out through Nature Preserve land and onto the ice of Lake Nubanusit, milky white, nine inches thick, and scumbled with the remains of previous snow blown across in freezing winds as the temperature went down last week. There was not a soul to be seen and my red jacket was the only color in a swirling landscape whose needle-sharp flakes fell at a sharp diagonal. I walked up to the head of the lake where Spoonwood's water was purling out under the granite blocks of the dam and making a small drinking hole—around which I could see the tracks of deer and moose. When I turned back the wind was in my face, and I could barely see my home shore. I thought of what it would be like to have a private fall through the ice at some spot where an underwater spring might have weakened the ice. I have never seen such spots on Lake Nubanusit, though I know they exist on other lakes. Three years ago a pickup truck went through on Nubanusit to the great amusement of locals. The driver had probably watched too many car ads on TV. A month later, when the ice was out, they got a cable on it and pulled it out, presumably to be sold as "a bargain." Anyhow, these thoughts brought me off the ice and back home before it became difficult to walk. All afternoon and evening the storm increased in force. Snow was falling at the rate of more than an inch an hour. The cats held to their positions around the wood stove, while the living room windows became blotched with snow, just the way that a third-grade teacher decorates her classroom for the Christmas play.

It snowed all night and was snowing when we got up. I woke during the dark hours and heard the rumble of plows and felt the house shake. The great orange leviathans, with one big plow on the front, and a side plow for knocking over mail boxes, bored along the King's Highway like the Supreme Court come to Settle an Election. The man who plows our driveway slipped in somewhere and plowed us out, so I was able to drive downtown to pick up the Times Sunday morning. There was an archetypal display! Plows to the left and plows to the right! Tired men sipping coffee in the cabs of their pickups, state plows with eight tons of sand on board and a little wheel at the back end to spin it all out on the road, men making the best of their snow blowers, old women crossing the road to church wrapped in white clouds like Venus calling on Aeneas. There were little bitty plows colored red and white, which one man could barely sit on, and enormous road graders that you stand up to steer like a ship—all turned out for action in this emergency that lifted everyone's spirits.

At the store, it was not necessary to mention the weather, because the thing spoke for itself. We all knew of the bad weather down south, and people had seen pictures on television of cars slithering off Interstates, but there was none of that in Hancock. The old ladies might have crossed the road at speed, but otherwise all was to be taken with slightly self-conscious aplomb.

February 2001

We have four wooden clocks in the house, none of them accurate. The clock repair man came last week and repaired two, which now work fairly well. The other two clocks, one on the porch and one in the basement, don't keep very good time. They are wood piles for the stove and supposedly say where winter is. The one on the porch says that we are in late March. The one in the basement (which also breeds ants) says that we are in mid-January. I shall try to adjust them next fall so as to keep closer time.

It's early afternoon, cold and sunny. This morning I walked for a couple of hours, following a trail through the woods that

I would not ordinarily be able to follow because of bugs and swamp, but which had been packed down pretty hard by yesterday's recreation. I turned into the woods across from Boutwell Road, went over a ridge and down to Route 123, which I crossed. The trail turned east and paralleled the road for a bit. I could hear cars passing. Then it rose gradually along an abandoned road through dense hemlock and after a while came out on the upper pasture of the Welch's farm. Then it veered left and rose through trees until I found myself standing on a town road with expensive houses all around me. It was time to turn back, so I did. Just across 123 I came across an unfortunate accident. A chipmunk had stored some of his nuts in the frame of an old metal bed. Coming out for breakfast his tongue had frozen to the frame (temperature 5 above this morning). I'm pretty sure this happened between the time I passed the bed on the way out and when I came back. He was quite frantic and there was frozen blood on the bedstead. Not thinking too clearly, but wanting to help I simply pulled him clear. He scampered off; I hope without serious damage.

The Ides of March, 2001

This was a bad day for Julius Caesar, but I have never had any trouble with it. I'm sitting in the basement, meditating the inevitability of death & taxes, the difficulty of the latter & possible difficulty of the former. I've certainly never heard of anyone ever accomplishing their taxes in a single stroke—as in falling off a roof. Which puts me in mind of shoveling snow off roofs.
I am going to have a look at the upper reaches of this house this afternoon, where a gigantic icicle has attached itself between the roof of the dormer and the lower roof. I will have to get up on a ladder and wrap my arms around it as if capturing a seal.
   I was reminded yesterday, while stepping casually from the slope of a snow pile onto the roof of the Nubanusit garage, of a story that might be true (vide Shel Silverstein) that a friend of

Albert's told me to enliven a bit of carpentry. It seems that a carpenter [he knew] went up to shovel snow off the roof one morning. It being rather high, he attached a safety rope to himself and tied the other end to the back of his pickup truck in front of the house. While he was at work on the far side of the roof, his wife came blearily out of the house, got into the truck and started to drive to the store for a dozen eggs. You can imagine his sensations on being jerked summarily over the rooftop. Fortunately, there was a grand pile of snow where he landed, so in no time, fully conscious, but quite disturbed, he found himself sliding down a snowy road on his back at 25 mph, trying to fend off small dogs and postboxes with his outspread legs. End of story, I'm afraid. He survived to tell the tale, and so, apparently, did she.

April 2001

We had a poetry read-around here last night for about six people. We met some interesting people, and plan to do it again at someone else's house in five or six weeks. In the meantime, I am planning to hike for a week or ten days on the Appalachian Trail in Virginia. I will start from Pammy's house in Virginia, and she will pick me up when I have had enough.

June 2001

Just learned that my poem "In Praise of English" will be published in a magazine called *Solo* later this summer. I probably have already showed it to you, but in case not, here it is.

In Praise of English

We can only offer you what you are—
Swart Saxon sounds,
Work of thingman and carl,
Labor of romance invaders,
Dash of sherbet, tomato, okra or punch.

Everywhere you are busy,
A hundred nations raise you up,
No longer of the one hearth,
But a favored person
With a thousand uncles.

We were born waiting for you,
Dearest—most free.
We suppose we remember you
Tucked away in the grains of our cells,
Yet cannot explain.

Every day you die, are reborn,
Put out shoots in improbable places,
Your secrets molder in grave sheets
And when you twitch the strings of our throats
We are astonished.

If we had not put aside making gods
We might worship you
Who are everywhere
Our closest companion
To the dumb-house of the Old Ones.

Did you know that my year at Exeter took place after I graduated from high school? Were it not for that year I would never have made it into Swarthmore. I had never had such good teachers, and had never cared for poetry until I had a class with a fellow named Claude Lloyd. He came from Texas, and was about my present age, his face was wrinkled and leathery, and for all I knew it had acquired that feature back in Texas when he was about ten. I had never before had a teacher who was able to ask a question and simply sit back and wait until someone was ready to answer. It is, in fact, one of the hardest things for teachers to do, and I have spent many fruitless classes attempting to master the method. In his class we read Browning, Yeats, Housman, Wallace Stevens and a fellow I had never even heard of named Gerard Manley Hopkins. Perhaps the best introduction to Hopkins would be one of the two or three of his poems we read for that class...

Pied Beauty

Glory be to God for dappled things—
   For skies of couple-color as a brinded cow;
      For rose-moles all in stipple upon trout that swim;
Fresh-firecoal chestnut-falls; finches' wings;
   Landscape plotted and pieced—fold, fallow, and plough;
      And all trades, their gear and tackle and trim.
All things counter, original, spare, strange;
   Whatever is fickle, freckled (who knows how?)
      With swift, slow; sweet, sour; adazzle, dim;
He fathers-forth whose beauty is past change:
   Praise him.

—G.M.H.

Hopkins was an odd fellow. Born in 1844 and died in 1889, he was a Victorian poet who made almost zero impression on his era. At the age of twenty-two he converted to Catholicism. This was a Big Deal at the time, as upper-class England was Anglican. In fact I believe that Catholics were not admitted to Oxford and Cambridge at the time. In any case, it meant abandoning a promising career that almost certainly would have involved a professorship at Oxford. Soon after his conversion, he joined the Jesuits (burning all his poetry up to that time). He served as a Parish priest (far below his abilities) and only began to write poetry again when his pastor suggested that it would be nice to have an elegy written for some nuns drowned at sea. In 1884, the order sent him to Dublin to teach Greek, where he died of typhoid fever five years later. He published almost nothing during his lifetime, and would have died without recognition had it not been for the efforts of a minor Victorian poet named Robert Bridges, who happened to become Poet Laureate of England. Hopkins' poems were first published in 1918, and by the time I came to Swarthmore, poetry teachers thought a lot of him. People pay less attention to him now and I think that is too bad. Late in life he had a spiritual crisis and wrote poems about his fear of losing religious faith. Here's one—and then I will cease torturing you...

> I wake and feel the fell of dark, not day.
> What hours, O what black hours we have spent
> This night! What sights you, heart, saw; ways you went!
> And more must, in yet longer light's delay.
>
> With witness I speak this. But where I say
> Hours I mean years, mean life. And my lament
> Is cries countless, cries like dead letters sent
> To dearest him that lives alas! away.
>
> I am gall, I am heartburn. God's most deep decree
> Bitter would have me taste: my taste was me;
> Bones built in me, flesh filled, blood brimmed the curse.

Selfyeast of spirit a dull dough sours. I see
The lost are like this, and their scourge to be
As I am mine, their sweating selves, but worse.

—G.M.H.

Four or five years ago a new biography of Hopkins came out,
and when I read it I wrote down some of the lines that turned
into [several drafts, becoming] the poem below. I think it helps
to have some idea of who the man was.

Gerard Manley Hopkins

Where you recognized a cross
you would clamber up
and consider the view,
not out of pride,
that fashionable oxidant,
but as crux innate
of your perilous calling.
Beauty must sear,
talent destroy, terror be ridden,
beggar give all...
'til the last crumb fall from the table.

2 September 2001

During WW II, my mother used to do her grocery shopping
at Rams' Market in Lee. It was the nearest town to Lenox with
both meat and grocery shopping, and since we had an A gas ra-
tion card, which meant the least allowance per week, the mere
two and a half miles was a country blessing. Lee was about as different from Lenox as could be. Where Lenox had thousand-acre
estates abandoned by their New York wealthies after the one-two
punch of the depression and the graduated income tax, Lee had

only the depression. It made the most of it. The factory along the Housatonic River closed down. There was little call for stone from the quarry, and the grubby main street was festooned with dank-looking bars and barely open shops. Rams' was a place of relative liveliness in that landscape. There, my mother could palaver with Mr. Rams himself, in his stained butcher's apron, confident that she was getting every last bit out of her meat coupons. Meanwhile, I was entranced by an automatic doughnut machine, whose doughnuts were extruded into a kind of merry-go-round of boiling oil and flipped over by a mechanical arm when they were halfway round. I do not remember Mother ever buying any, despite my protestations. Jonathan, my little brother aged six or seven, went directly to the cookies, which were displayed in little open barrels directly beneath the counter. He would open their glass fronts and help himself when Mother's attention was distracted.

6 October, 2001

Your Mom and I are still sleeping on the porch. There was a pretty good wind last night and the oak trees were firing off salvos of acorns (this is a big acorn year). When I got up at 5:30 the moon was bright in the west and the sky was clear. But soon clouds came on and the wind picked up. Rain was pretty sure, so I hurried to get some more wood in the basement, drawing on the pile at the head of the driveway. Then to the dump, and home just as the rain began. I made and put up 2 1/2 quarts of green tomato chutney and also immersed basil and some Vietnamese plant we have been growing in vinegar.

I'm listening to Bach's Peasant Cantata (which makes me think of drinking beer). The music is really quite lovely.

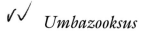

Umbazooksus

Tourists and ranger gone home,
An old fellow in a red hat
Fishing from a beat canoe
Vanishes in falling snow.

There are no dead letters to God, Gerard
It who is the Great Postman on high
and who gathers all words to its plate
and buckles on armor [of wine.]
But is this a message of hope, sly,
Or only a sop to despair?

[*handwritten*]

Earth is not my home.
It's just where my bones are
moving around
till they're sent down,
and where they will lie
for a pretty long time.

Where is the smell,
where is the sound
of my town?
It isn't above
or in this ground.

My home is somewhere else.

Words to the Same End
I. House of Mercy Hospital

Hearing the crows' raucous voices,
Seeing them rise from branches
In the gathering dusk of late October,
Muted in this ruby moment,
Black against amethyst;
Oh, dark fruits,
Disobedient to gravity—
Like applause hanging
Over a dumb stadium
Or a miasma of bats
Blown from the unbelievable lungs
Of a swart cave—
Recalling a far invitation;
A sick man takes his words
Into the gape of gape...
"No prayer is wasted."

II. Don't Ask

Don't ask, I know
Where words go....
Up from the tranquil wood
Like dark fruit, gleaming,
They rise, those careless ravens,
To far invitations
Winging, laughing.
No prayer is wasted.

Ludwig Wittgenstein Meets Chuang-Tzu

They are talking about
what can be talked about,
watching "Easy Street,"
drinking black tea.
There's a shimmer of amber's
rubbed crackling in the air.

They are talking about
what can be talked about
in flats and pavilions
of banked roses and butterflies.
The hems of their shirts
are stitched in stories
in which the other appears
unpocketing paradoxes.

They are talking about
what can be talked about.
They are discussing
things undiscoverable,
while their disciples
take notes at side tables.

If their eyes had met
you would have thought
something might have been said
for which no word suffices,
but the thing they attempt,
which cannot be said,

enables the hearing of something
else, which has nothing to do
with the question.

The piping of heaven?

6

❧ Cleaning the face of morning

Dear Ali,

I have been boiling sap, as the attached little sheet describes. It started out as an email explanation of my doings, but developed into something that might be publishable. It will only be viable for a short time more, as the maple syrup season ends soon. We put out 31 taps this year, which is too many, so I have been putting in twelve hour days at the stove two or three times a week. I think that we may end by calling an early halt when we have as much as we can use and bottle for gifts.

Since it is March we are sugaring in the back yard. Our thirty maple taps each dangle a plastic milk jug, marking time in droplets. We boil on an old barrel stove fished from the dump. Tom Paquette at Fran's Autobody cut out the top and made a base for the pans from a bed rail. A day's boiling makes two quarts of syrup, but there was a freeze last night so I skimmed the barrels this morning. The ice is lacy or mushy, depending on the temperature, and sticks to the ground all day. Skimming ice makes for richer sap and more syrup. While sugaring is kind of pastoral and lazy in theory, the fact is its leisures are few, barely enough to get a grip on spring training or read a few paperback pages.

Back to the syrup. Up at 5 am, fire lit by quarter of six, boil in twenty minutes, then time for a cup of coffee. Split and add wood, being careful not to smother the heat, skim froth from the pans because it covers the boil and reduces evaporation—later on it will taste sweet. Out to the garage. Pour five-gallon bucket through sieve into empty bucket. Ice from garbage barrel reservoir. Bucket to fire, pour through sieve into large metal pitcher. Throw out more ice and a snow flea. Lid on pitcher, place on concrete block next to fire box to warm. Skim froth. Split more wood. Balance army cup full of sap next to stove pipe—more pre-heating. Drive downtown for paper etc., etc.

Lunch on hot dog pierced with ceiling hanger wire and suspended next to fire box. Roll warmed in mess cup. Baste with hot syrup. Relax. Lean back in metal chair (found with stove). Watch sky—cloudless blue—branches stirring in smart breeze. Glimpse young otter grooming on pond ice. Feel stove heat on face, sun on back... Gooood! Now, then. Up! Up! Skim froth, split wood, add sap, etc., etc.

4 p.m. Time to stop adding sap. What! Are you crazy? Lots of time yet! O.K., 4:30. Watch final boil. Balance syrup in pans for maximum evaporation. Start using candy thermometer. Syrup done at seven degrees above water boil. Water here boils around 211 degrees. We're shooting for 220 and thicker syrup. Not rocket science, but we don't want to have a sugar spasm, end up with rock candy in the pan. Ah! 217 degrees. It won't be long now. Time to combine pans. Pay attention. Return empty pan with plain water to keep draft in stove and ash from remaining pan. This syrup will have a faint smoky flavor.

Pan starts to boil up! Maple Nymph curses uppity novice? Shout magic charm, "Butter! Butter! Where's the butter?" Chuck in tiny piece. Nymph pacified. (Can taste butter behind smoke? No. Can taste iron crowbar used to loosen ice in barrel? No. Too bad.) Situation tense. Check temperature. 219 degrees. Will be 220 in a minute. Don't be fooled. Time for final skim. Thick white scum tastes delicious. Tiny flecks of ash good for what ails you.

Ah ha! Magic number, 220. Count to thirty, place sieve on pitcher, pull on heavy gloves. This syrup is thick and honey-colored and has many small bubbles rising in such a slow hurry. Which corner of the pan has the least carbon? That's the one to pour from. The syrup bursts out in a golden flood as it dives into the pitcher—like glorious blowout at end of fireworks. Toss out gray residue in the bottom of pan. Clap cover on pitcher, head for house. Sunset glow is in the west. The stars are out. There are plane lights over the mountain. Clean up the instruments and have a glass of beer with syrup in it.

I'm back here after only two days on the trail, but having had a very good visit with Pam and Wayne. The trail turned out to be too much for me, mainly because I had not done sufficient physical preparation (stair climbing), but also because I hadn't thought carefully enough about what I was getting into and had made equipment mistakes in my concern to lighten my pack. The biggest mistake was to take a light sleeping bag, in which I shivered at 30 degrees my one night in a shelter. There I met a man who had encountered fifteen degrees a couple of days before at 3,500 feet (where I was headed). As I clumb up and down hill on a day that ultimately reached 85 degrees in cloudless weather, I decided that I wasn't prepared for the worst I might encounter, so hitched a ride with an elderly couple from Texas along Skyline Drive back to my start. Pam picked me up the next day within a couple of miles of where she had let me off, and the following day I drove back here in one fell swoop.

I thought you might be amused by a journal entry from my [earlier] hike on the Trail, which I have been spiffing up:

Toads on the Trail

9 August The trouble begins, as Mark Twain would have it, soon after sundown. At Race Brook Falls campsite, where I spent last night, the text was given out in twilight. "Ask!" proposed some old tree frog (or toad as the case may be). And after a thoughtful pause, "Ask" again. Then with gradually increasing tempo over the space of five minutes or so, "Ask! Ask! ASK! ASK!ASK!" Finally, like someone winding up an argument before the Supreme Court, a solemn reversal, "Ask NOT!"

And here comes a second voice, just as near, "ASK!" calls the second, perhaps supporting, maybe contradicting the first. A third, fourth, more speakers enter in—to and fro, back and forth. The whole thing becomes a kind of fugue tumbling over itself; sometimes in concord, at other times a mere hash of sound. Another word enters: "WHAT!", now interrogative, now exclamatory, now dazed. These complications are hard to follow after a long day and soon shuffle me off to sleep.

I surface around midnight into a Hector Berlioz dream. The fugue has become an enormous symphony with a vast series of individual choruses, each more distant from my tent, but still distinct in a rough and ready way. Dissonances resonate into consonance, and the whole is weaving itself into a vast quilt that covers the dark woods with shimmering sound. So various are the voices, and so ambiguous, that without willing it my mind imposes its own libretto on them. "ASK," it says, "ASK NOT!" "ASK NOT WHAT?" "ASK NOT WHAT YOU CAN DO FOR YOUR COUNTRY! ASK WHAT YOUR COUNTRY CAN DO FOR YOU!" The riposte is that silver thread, "ASK NOT WHAT YOUR COUNTRY CAN DO FOR YOU, BUT WHAT YOU CAN DO FOR YOUR COUNTRY."

For some time I listened in a half doze to this operatic debate—like the court recorder who gets it all down without paying attention. Then I drifted off again. By four o'clock the frogs had packed it in. Already crickets were cleaning the face of morning.

October 2002

It's 8:30 in the morning of one of those warm, gray, wet mornings that you sometimes get in October. The colors huddle on the trees across the pond, hoping that no big wind will come up to blow them off before they show what they can do in full sunlight.

✓

[Out making syrup]

On even a calm day the branches ripple
in the heat of the stove pipe and a little
nimbus of visual uncertainty lies
around the barrel of the stove.

[*handwritten*]

✓

Haiku

What sudden applause
Surprises dawn-smooth water?
Two loons taking off.

Gluck
(On a line from Anthony Hecht)

Not very lucky
were you, Heinrich,
kinsman of Heine,
to have me in your class,
a small-town kid from
Vermont who knew
Old Testament,
but little of the outer world.
Jews were glorious folk
who took the foreskins
of their enemies, and
directions from wild Prophets
off hills like mine
to set them straight.

I found your accent strange,
your interest in the ways
of rats confined to mazes
stranger than your accent.
In such a world I bobbed,
a half-soaked cork,
until mid-term when
you set me straight.
Your office hour I soon
provoked, exam in hand,
and learned from you
how little I approached
The Discipline.

It must have tempted
you, my gormlessness,
a veritable provocation.
Soon, soon, were telling me
those words in spate, the Holocaust,
all smoking hot,
not from The Book, but family;
stoked with corrosive guilt
I now surmise.
(How could you have
the luck to live when died,
Died Horribly, those close and far.)
I left, not comprehending
my shame and anger, and
bearing some of yours.
I thought of you thereafter as
"Un-professor Gluck."

How is it that your ghost
is sitting with me here
and speaking in my mind
the still small words?

Now rats are everywhere,
some caged, some running free,
but where are prophets?
The Lord of Hosts, His
ironies on fire,
casts back and forth,
now branding one,

now laying down a maze that
few can solve and
none can understand.
Oh Mister If—
Whose cold by day,
Whose fire by night
We'd have preside,
send us more light,
"More light! More light!"

Faith ✓✓   *bit d Jay's scepticism*

Yes! Faith is that gravity
Against which we rise
With which we contend—
Like spaceships
Like motorcycles in a
Carnival barrel,
Round and round,
Higher and higher
Seeking that sea
Of nothing where
Only tiniest things
And worlds imagined
Exist.

Who uproots himself
Flies against faith,
Explorer and ————-
To perish searching
For that which is.

"That which is, is,
and not some other thing."

[*handwritten*]

Triptych

Faith is the root
From which we rise
And distant, leaf
In air, not earth

Longer we live
Further we grow
Less and less know
What feeds below.

When the leaves fall
Separately, all
Into the earth,
Feeding the root

What does it know,
Swelling below,
Heeding the word,
"Grow simply grow."

It's hard to hope
Swimming in unison
I hope I never have to hope,
But sometime it will come
Upon me when I am
Defenseless—

And I will not resent it
But accept what I
Cannot control,
As stranded sailors
Accept the rising tide.

Charity is the simple one
Asking only that we act,
Ceding intent.
Put aside the acquisition of merit,
Purification will
Find its own way,
Adjust your step
To the heart's great drum.

deeper! then maybe winter longing.

Exhortation: To Prayer

Do not bend over
Like the exhausted rower
Who leans on his oar,
But put your back into it—
Trunk, arms, calf, spine
As on the return.

Do not modulate your voices
Shriek, sigh, grunt, blow praise into a handkerchief,
All willful noise is praise,
Whether you know it or not.

Do not stand or kneel composedly,
But saunter or stretch
Butterfly fashion,
Like the linebacker about
To pounce
Or the windsurfer
Delicately aware
Of the wind's foible.

Have no incense before you,
But snuff the raw mist
For the faintest note
Of the divine essence;
Hunter or hunted
Hunter or hunted.

Do these things
Because they are there to be taken;
The surfer's wave,
The butterfly's avenue/

> Amen

*Walter's NELP class prepares to
meet on Mount Chocorua*

Watching a NELP performance

*Walter and Francelia
camping on
Moosehead Lake*

Walter, Jonathan, Francelia at home, Hunt's Pond

Francelia and Alison, Hunt's Pond

On Nubanusit Lake

Her parents return for Alison's University of Michigan graduation

"Incompetent woodsman at work here"

Alison, home for Christmas

"Let it rise for another hour, bake and taste. Good, eh?"

"Skim froth. Split more wood."

Raising the home garage, with Ira Dole and Tim Benson

Raising the Sawyer Farm barn, Jaffrey

Alison and Walter on the Ammonoosuc Trail, Mount Washington

Brothers under trees planted at their births, Lenox, Massachusetts

With Jonathan and his son David, and Kineo

With Walter's cousin Linda Murray, Lake Wentworth

Visiting on the porch, Nubanusit

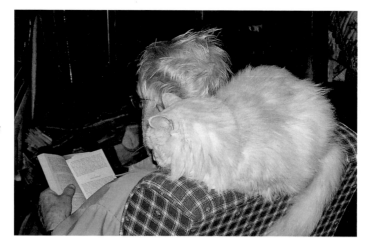

Reading with Rafie

In teaching mode

Listening

Awaiting the pick-up plane, St. John River, Maine

7

∽ Generally getting warm

Dear Ali,

Happy New Year!

Last night we went to Nelson for their New Years Eve Pot Luck and Contra Dance. We arrived around 7:20, bearing a cauldron of pea soup and found the field already hotly engaged. There were about a hundred people in the high-ceilinged Nelson Community Hall, a no-nonsense space with hard-to-open windows, lights hanging down on stiff rods and trestle tables on saw horses around the edges. Shelf paper had been unrolled on the tables, and all manner of food deposited thereon, amongst which our humble soup felt no need to be shy. Picking and choosing among various dishes, we filled our paper plates and picked up plastic implements. Francelia has been mixing with some of the town's artists (there are enough so that they have a small communal shop, where Francelia displays some of her work and also serves time behind the cash register on weekends). I was introduced to some of the artists, and others were pointed out to me. People milled about the central space, gnawed chicken bones along the sidelines, or called to some among the many small children who skittered about in that special way children have on ski slopes, ice rinks and dance floors. After a while the sound system began to laboriously assemble itself at the hands of guitarists, electricians, high school kids, piano players and fiddlers. The trestle tables were dismantled and leftover food shoved under benches. The guitar began to play one reel and the fiddle another, while the piano player adjusted his chair just so.

In no time the caller, tall and disheveled, stepped to the mike, and each father grabbed a daughter, each mother a son, the smaller the better, except for infants. They were unceremoniously tucked in amongst buffalo wings and platters of spicy tofu under the tables. Before we knew it we were spinning about in confusion, our arms full of young tikes and aged grandparents, for whose bones and aches we had a care, promenading, swinging our corners, etc., etc., and generally getting warm. The caller was good (i.e. comprehensible and undemanding) and we had three good sets, at which point the parents whisked the children away with an almost magical lack of commotion. A new caller, fiddler and pianist replaced the first group and both pace and difficulty stepped up. We lasted through a set or two of this (I with the help of strangers, Francelia with no help from me, I fear), watched a set and then called it quits. I had the sense that quite a few young adults were leaving about the time we did—bound for private parties. Meanwhile the professionals (who could be recognized by their dancing pumps and ponytails) were just getting serious. I'm sure that the figures that followed must have put DNA to shame.

February 2003

The thermometer has been doing its thing! This morning the temperature at the back door was minus ten degrees, and I was briefly tempted to head out to the Fiddlehead Café, which advertises free ice cream at minus five and below. (We've already had a pint of their homemade ice cream at half price—sold when the temperature gets below 15+.) Things have warmed up to 10 above by this writing. Both wood stoves are going full blast and the cats are keeping close to them. I was out walking the day before yesterday in similar weather. The wind was howling in the treetops, and fleecy clouds, as they say, were tearing across the sky. My pace and clothing kept me warm—and I rediscovered what was learned in a study of Norwegian fishermen, namely that if the hands are active, they can warm up even in the coldest conditions. This is actually one of my favorite times of year. The snowmobiles open trails on the weekend that lead to the unlikeliest places, swamps and views from high up that you would never get to in summer time. If the wind is not too bad I hope to find good walking at Pitcher Mountain in Stoddard, which is crossed by a hiking trail that goes from Monadnock to Mt. Sunapee.

I was drinking coffee the other morning and looking idly at the pond—watching the ice thicken—when a fox suddenly came into view. It was about fifty yards off shore and moving rapidly from right to left. Little taller than Jefferson, and probably lighter, it had something in its jaws and was twinkling along at a good pace, not loping, for the ice was slippery. I called your mom, and we watched it for what seemed like a long time, though it could not have been more than a minute. Quite a gift! It's not that foxes are rare, one can see their tracks all around. The Bickfords, who live on Route 123, had the pleasure of a den in their back yard for two years running and could watch the cubs playing in the spring. But foxes are shy and you are more apt to catch a glimpse of one at the edge of the road, or disappearing over a stone wall.

March 2003

Today is one of those warm clear days of which we have not had ANY since some time in November. We have been deploying maple taps for the past couple of weeks to little effect, perhaps eight gallons of sap frozen solid in the collecting buckets. I went walking up the road with pickax and shovel to dig out a path to our last tree this morning. It's just off the road and there is solid ice to go through where the plows had mounded the snow, with surprisingly soft corn snow underneath. After cutting a path I went in to the tree and drilled two holes about 2 ½ inches deep with a hand drill, stuck taps in place and hammered them lightly in with a hammer. As I went back to the truck to get a couple of plastic milk jugs (what we use for buckets), my eye was caught by a flash of moving water at the side of the road. A veritable flash flood was just beginning on the south side of the road (normally protected) where the early morning sun had started thawing the banks. I watched with approval as the little tide swept down the side of the road. Like the ice going out on the pond it was certifiable proof that spring was on the way. Your mother is riding with a friend this morning and as I write, Rafie is lying out in languorous fashion on the side deck. This last is perhaps an even more powerful proof of spring, since for most of the winter Rafie has responded to open doors with marked aversion.

Later this afternoon I shall go out and put the dilapidated drum stove up on its concrete feet, and try once more to fit its homemade door onto the latches. I have already scoured out the two lasagna pans which serve as evaporators. They are the weak link in my springtime extravaganza and I shall be hoping for something new next year.

May 2003

We have moved the sofa out onto the porch and converted it into a bed. Lately the weather has been cool and wet—very Seattle—and this morning as I was waking up there was a lovely conflation of three sounds; rain on the roof, peepers down where the wetland runs into the lake, and birds unidentifiable in the woods. There is a ravens' nest somewhere between us and the neighbors, but they are uncharacteristically quiet. One sees large black bodies negotiating their way through the upper branches of trees on the way to some undisclosed destination. Perhaps we will hear in due time the sound of young birds. I remember describing baby herons as sounding like a knitting factory.

We have two new cherry trees (pie variety, i.e. sour) and a couple more dwarf pear trees. Perhaps we will start to get some negotiable fruit in the next few years. Of the dozen blueberries I planted two years ago, one has given up the ghost to voles, but eleven are flourishing and it looks as if we will have some for the freezer this year, as well as fruit cups, pies and on breakfast cereal. Four rows of peas are already above ground, their tendrils reaching for the wire fence. Broccoli is in, but not looking especially happy, and I have tomato plants ready to go in later this week. The peonies look very promising, as do some lilies that arrived late last year with a lovely scent. I'll soon put out our battered Rosemary and Basil plants.

Off now to read Walt Whitman's *Song of Myself*, as am reading it aloud next week with some other people at the Hancock Library.

It's early afternoon on one of those cool sunny July days, dealt so sparingly from the weatherman's pack—wind from the northwest and dry. Tonight we will go down to the low sixties or high fifties, another escape from the heat of summer. The red truck is into the shop for a thorough overhaul, so after your mom left for a session with Shush, I strolled up to the woodlot and split, hauled and stacked for a while in the cool of the morning, then gathered blueberries for jam, two small bottles of which are cooling on the stove as I write. After I take this up to the mailbox there's some heavy weeding to be done in the garden, then perhaps I'll get back to the woodlot, or just take things easy for a while. Such is the life of retirement.

Saw two young wildcats on 123 about six in the morning the other day. They have high back ends like miniature poodles. I do not think they could have been anything else. Were wandering about as if lost, but skedaddled back into the undergrowth as the car got closer.

A picture of the Vermont State Archivist wearing a Hawaiian shirt caught my eye the other day. Woke up in the middle of the night and thought of the idea of a Hawaiian shirt with beard painted on it (and perhaps a complementary T-shirt with beard so that you wouldn't have to sacrifice the collar). Theme would be Edward Lear limerick . . . .

> There was an old man with a beard
> Who said "It is just as I feared;
>   Two owls and a hen,
>   Four larks and a wren,
> Have all made their nests in my beard."

Shirt could have the limerick in small print here and there. Birds peeping out of palm trees. Palm trees with beards on top instead of palms. Little cars with larks driving, or old men driving and birds covering their eyes with wings. Steal W.C. Fields joke—old man in driver's seat has wheel in hands. He's taken it off the steering rod and is about to hand it to a large owl in passenger seat. Sketch of Lear (is there one by Max Beerbohm?) somewhere on shirt. Birds from bird book sketched here and there. Perfect for Alan Howes. Advertise in *Audubon* magazine?

November 2003

I had my coffee this morning in front of the living room window so I could watch the first sun catch the tops of the trees to the west. After a while a solitary laggard duck flew off from somewhere to the right and presently an otter appeared who was working the shoreline. His head bobbed up a few times, and then I could see his broad back as he scouted for possible fish, and then he was gone. The protected bits of inshore pond have their first thin covering of ice, which will melt later today. This is one of my favorite times—at least when it isn't raining or snowing. The bones of the land can be seen, and there are places that invite you to walk in which are masked with a solid wall of greenery during the summer. The enormous oak at the turn in the driveway near the house, which we had taken down about six weeks ago, has now been split and hauled up to the woodlot, where it added about a foot to the pile I am working on.

Haiku

Middle night—waking—

earthquake—the bedstead shaking—

cat scratching—maybe.

All night crickets sang
In the basement while eating
Pages of music

Puzzled Dust

Proud, angry, puzzled dust,
if led to water you may drink,
if beauty winks at you, you wink
but cannot comprehend the thrust
that tickles in your threaded bone;

bone dropped aside to flake and rust,
return to elemental grist
while ghost goes where you cannot guess.
Some say it goes to study trust—
ing earth as if that were its home

and it, when ready, also might return.
In any case, by then you're gone.
Whatever sticks it might pick up again
are not your creamy meal and bone,
long since locked up in stubborn stone.

But who would ever ask the dust
to name the height of its desire,
"Lift or be lifted somewhat higher?"
The summonsed earth need not atone
for being but the ground of song.

"Isn't": Two Routes to the Same Hut

"That which is, is and not some other thing."
Bishop Berkeley

But George, those other things are what
I mostly seem to crave, the world so flawed
Given the choice to never do without
I'd be a moment in the mind of God.
For if, as they say, instants are eras there
Your *isn't* is what I can't do without.
Not having faith, you say, negates my prayers
Which hold all things that are suspect
But like some mathematic reject
Explore the asymptotic of sublime.

Hyphen! I loved word & period to devotion to God!

②

[*handwritten*]

Prayer

Why bother?

At the extremities things alter
Cold fingers unable to grasp may still drum
Deaf ears imagine the trills of awakening toads
Isolates on horseback,
Shipboard at the edge of the city
Desert fathers to whom come
Visitors in alternate decades;
May they not dream the wishes eternal?

Harsh labor, fasting, weather extreme
These honor the mind
attentive to pain and privation.
Furrows and folds lie open
seeds innumerable borne on the winds
of the galaxy from systems unnameable,
as if the unfolding universe were to
shoot spores ahead of itself only
to gather them up in what we call mind
of this marginal being whose
address on a side street of a
minority of a provincial galaxy
is nevertheless a crevice in time
to bear a strange flowering.

II. So the universe thinks itself?

How egotistical.
But that separation we
humans take as a given:

[98]

the self-aware mind examining itself.
What an achievement for a cosmic explosion.
Impossible to imagine an atomic
explosion begetting a legion of
infinitesimal admirers no
matter how brief their span.

This alone is reason for prayer.

III. And does it matter?

Need it matter any more than
the myriad purposes of the
infinitesimal beings who see
themselves in the terrifying
mirror of —————————.

*human worship
(or admire
creation —
nature — and
Atoms!*

[*handwritten*]

Three

Looking Outward

2004–2007

WALTER'S WRITING BROADENS AND BOTH FORMS HOST his sense of humor. His letters to Alison show him deflecting his anger at politics with humor, as well as filtering his own fatherly advice through the pen of Solzhenitsen. Describing our visit to Puerto Rico, he casts himself as the unruly guest. At home, he shows that we were always riveted to the spot by the privilege of our views of wildlife.

He has revised three earlier poems, *The Prince, Messenger,* and *They Were Traveling,* but most of his energy is new. The humor in the new ones suggests a comfortable, large resolution, as does the scope of subjects from the army, to dreams of northern Canada, to home. *Memorial Day at the Robert Frost Campground,* in addition to its salty voice of Frost, is a reminder that Walter was still teaching classes in the "rumble seat" of NELP. *Finish Me,* 2004, which shows his intent for his handwritten poems on the shelf, is the only clue to their presence. A couple of years later, he had created half a dozen more of them. Now the two handwritten poems about death are the two most humorous ones: *Room C 2J,* inspired by finding his army dog tag, and *Death by Custard,* so hard for the spouse to swallow.

Alison by now was living in Boston, and we were seeing her often. I had become steady in my art projects and my horse project. Walter had become a library trustee, and he shared in reading poetry from northern New England regularly. Together with these readers, he had accumulated a "fan club" by word of mouth.

Twenty-five years before in Ann Arbor, when Walter was turning fifty, he mused to me, "The second half of life is like coming down a mountain. You have left the summit, but you know the trail and you know exactly how beautiful it is, know what you appreciate most. So the descent can be seen as the most beautiful part of the climb." The last two poems are about this kind of descent.

— F. M. C.

8

ও Where to stick and where to let go

January 2004

Dear Ali,

Happy New Year! Last night I watched the Patriots beat the Tennessee Titans, and this morning am cutting wood. Since the temperature hovers around zero and the sun is not out, I have to come in every hour or two to warm up and get a hot drink of some sort, so I thought I'd write a quick note while the process is underway.

As you know, my retirement hobbies include not only despoiling the forest and advising my daughter (do I have the order right?), but also wasting my time with books. The Hancock Library got in a book about relations between Churchill and Roosevelt during WW II. I glanced at it doubtfully, feeling that the field was one that had been well gleaned, but it drew me in and I am now about halfway through. It gives a lot of the little things (relations with servants, for instance—or Churchill's role as the one seeking, and Roosevelt's role as the distant, sought-after one). Incidentally, some American diplomat, politician or cabinet member who had a fairly close-up view of Roosevelt is quoted in the book as saying that Roosevelt was personally completely cold and unattractive, though capable of putting on a good show—but that he was an absolutely superb president. That was a thought-provoking remark for me.

I enclose the latest version of a poem I am working on that has to do with maple syrup. My problem is not to let it get too much like Robert Frost, although I am willing to allow him to get his nose under a corner of the tent.

First Run

This February syrup in its jar
Is gift too precious to go far,
Tea-pale as an evening sky
That shows a crescent moon in place;
Not to be entered at the Fair
Or nailed for glory to the sugar wall,
It asks what we should make of rare:
Run down from it through A, B, C,
To the very bottom root of tree
(Home of the skittering snow flea)
Or sip from coffee spoons at will?

I know that some would spurn it all,
One spoonful being enough, a grace
Too sweetly perfect for a meal,
As if to sip such drops of air
Gave promise of some rarer rare
Not reachable by human minds,
Just as the moon hung out on high
Makes cold enigma in the sky.

But as for me, I drink to Jean
(Who boiled, out behind the barn,
And finished on his kitchen stove
This ordinary gift for friends)
A child's cup of springing life.

An interesting thing I am doing is preparing for a live poetry reading with some other people. It is tentatively scheduled for late summer or early fall at the Hancock Library. The theme is birds or flight and we are at the stage now of sending one another poems for consideration. Here are a couple of haiku that I like...

> The butterfly
> Resting upon the temple bell,
> Asleep.   Buson

> On the temple bell
> Glowing,
> A firefly.   Shiki

Yesterday morning was cold and gray, but the pond was clear and smooth. Drinking my coffee in typical idle fashion, I looked out to see what was stirring. There was a loon in the middle of the pond, and shortly after, another. They swam slowly past one another, dipping their beaks. "Aha," thought I, "courtship." I had been wondering for some time whether there were enough fish in the pond to support a breeding pair. The water stays level because of the dam, and this means a lot to loons, who can't walk on land. If the water level falls during incubation, the nest can be left high and dry. Since the loon population in southwest New Hampshire has been expanding at a good clip, I supposed that they might be thinking of building a nest. I was just blessing the wedding when a third loon showed up, then a fourth, then a fifth. Five loons together are not unusual to see in the fall, when there are communal gatherings before migration, but I had never seen five loons together on Hunt's Pond before, even in the fall. It seemed very odd—and remains odd, for I have only guesses and questions to offer. If the original pair were nesting, then there was not yet an egg in the nest, or they would not both have been out together. Also, I believe that bill dipping can be a court-ship rite. But what about the other three loons? Could they have been juveniles? Just visiting? Wouldn't the male of a nesting pair attempt to drive the others off? It made no sense. Furthermore the five loons as a whole seemed to engage in what I think of as "social swimming," which includes not only bill dipping, but also mutual diving, and inspections of the underwater area while others are diving. Your mom looked too, and found it equally mysteri-ous. After a while there was the kind of rapid swim-walking and standing on end that signify excitement and (often) aggression.

When I looked for loons this morning there were none. Per-haps there will be further developments.

I found a copy of one of Solzhenitsen's novels at Wolfeboro last week and brought it home with me to read. I came across the following speech, which is addressed by an older, more expe-rienced political prisoner to a young scientist who is imprisoned in the same "research" prison.

"How to face difficulties?" he declared again. "In the realm of the unknown, difficulties must be viewed as hidden treasure! Usually, the more difficult, the better. It's not as valuable if your difficulties stem from your own inner struggle. But when difficul-ties arise out of increasing objective resistance, that's marvelous!"

The rosy dawn now shone on his flushed face as if conveying the radiance of difficulties wonderful as the sun.

"The most rewarding path of investigation is: 'the greatest external resistance in the presence of the least internal resist-ance.' Failures must be considered the cue for further applica-tion of effort and concentration of will power. And if substantial efforts have already been made, the failures are all the more joyous. It means that our crowbar has struck the iron box con-taining the treasure. Overcoming the increased difficulties is all the more valuable because in failure the growth of the person performing the task takes place in proportion to the difficulty encountered!"

"Good! Strong!" Nerzhin responded from the pile of firewood.

There's an old joke about the fellow who read Hemingway and went off to fight bulls in Spain, which warns against taking literature as a guide to life. But the best literature gives us stuff to think about, to take or leave as we deem pertinent. And literature is, in a way, life cleaned up. Where to stick and where to let go, when to hold 'em and when to fold 'em—these seem to me to be the very stuff of the difficulties you are facing now.

June 2004

The "Nubie News" reports that the eagles which have nested here and there around the lake have gone back to one of their old nests, and now have three fledglings. If they make it through to adulthood they will be the first from this pair.

As you know, things have been pretty wild up until a couple of days ago. First I joined a NELP smorgastrip in Middlebury, where we visited Frost's cabin during the years he spent summers in Ripton, Vermont. It's quite small, almost shabby, and is about a hundred yards from a real farmhouse, where he used to get his meal. There is a lovely view across mowed fields to mountains to the southwest. I camped out in my hiking tent, and the next day we all went to the special library at Dartmouth where they have a Frost collection. The students looked at pictures, and at some of his notebooks. I drove home that evening and spent the next day getting ready for our trip to Swarthmore and my 50th college reunion.

July 2004

Got up early this morning—earlier than I wanted—as can happen during the summer months. The atmosphere today is like a shower stall used by many, although the rain is holding off. This morning I drove off early to pick blueberries at a place in Troy. Normally the place has a lovely view to the northeast, but today things were cool and clammy. I parked and picked up a pail, walked down a grassy aisle to a recommended row and began to pick. The berries, which were the size of grapes, hung in great clusters and I could pick five at a time (a handful), pausing only to pick out stems and leaves.

When I found a bush where the berries tasted good I stayed for a while. Some of them actually had a slight honey taste. I tried to avoid the biggest ripest ones, because I wanted some of that tart quality that you want in a winter pie, or to solidify blueberry/ginger jam. There were a few birds and a few children to be heard, the latter at just the right distance. Every so often a terrific bird racket would break out, sounds of distress as if some bird were being squeezed to death. These, it turns out, were recorded distress cries, played back over the hi-fi to discourage predation. Judging from the size of the berries and the fullness of the bushes it must have worked. When I congratulated the owner on my way out he excused himself by saying that it had been a very wet spring. It's been a very wet spring here, but none of the bushes in our backyard have anything like such a load.

August 2004

Yesterday I was up early, and in due time down to the market to get the day's paper and to meet briefly with the newly installed parrot on the front porch of the Inn. As is my wont, I repeated three times in a quiet, but firm voice, Flush Bush, Flush Bush, in hope that it will come to flower in time for election day.

October 2004

Down town early this morning for the paper. I got there about ten minutes before the store opened and spent the time walking up and down on the sidewalk. A number of houses are being repaired, and I could see stacked furniture, paint cans and piles of lumber through those old New England windows. It was actually a little weird when you stop to think that the turnover in these houses is high. Well-to-do officers of big companies retire here, and pay a lot for the houses as well as some more to have them brought to a high inside glaze. They soon discover that downtown Hancock is relatively noisy, with traffic early and late, and not too many attractions beyond the store, the post-office and perhaps supper at the Inn. So the house is up for sale again after a few Thanksgivings and they are off to Florida or one of those real estate places where one is gently eased from one's own apartment by a series of stages into round-the-clock-care at considerable expense. When the store opened, I grabbed my paper and hurried back here.

The NELP reunion was a big success: 130 people showed up, including George (there was a contra-dance the first night) and other people you would have enjoyed talking to. It served to create some enthusiasm for further NELP fundraising, so I have been busy with that since I got back. Did take time for four days on the Appalachian Trail in Western Mass. One more such trip and I will have finished Mass. and Conn.—not much, but something.

Moon

In the cinema
of night's projection
leaves dancing
like motes in the beam.

They Were Traveling

And as night fell
came to the circle of unworked stone
by the scorched ogham
with the cracked bowl at its foot.

One tied the horse's hobble,
the other loosed the suggan,
threw down the cloth saddle
& pig's bladder of boiled pulse.

The same dream that night
came to each, the bowl
complete again, hand-shiny,
offering miraculous sup.

At dawn, fellowed in awe,
they silently saddle
and leave, one seated,
one trotting before.

The Prince

In the kitchen
The wrinkled woman told him stories.
They lived on beets,
But sent him to school where others
Told him who he was
And why he had been sent
To this out of the way place.

Believing it was a message,
He minded his manners
And the ways of the man and the woman;
And he was not surprised
When the owl spoke to him in the forest,
But assembled his scrip and left.

It was a mere county fair,
Still, he kept his head
and passed the tests with distinction,
only to find himself in the field
with a command unasked for,
people and states of affairs to assess.
It was all a great dream
And only the early hardships
Sustained him.

Then triumph hardly imagined
Surrounded him like a wet dream.
He was interviewed, feted
And cordoned off from the peasants;
Became a toy of the rich.

In the feather bed of night
things done, lives taken and maimed,
tactical lies told
circled around him in weird galliard
and Misery's Pomp placed
the circlet of Pain on his head.

For a while he bore it
As a hero should,
But then did that thing
Unimagined in the many stories
The woman had told him, — *his mother*
Removing the crown,
Placing himself under orders *students?*
to those he had ordered, refusing all challenges
But those of the orderly room or parade.

Did he live happy again?
Who can say *just a job*
That youthful ecstasy precludes
Comfort in middle age?
robust He felt he owed a debt to life —
thrust And tried to pay
When no familiar came to show the way

Let anyone who can
Write down an ending
On the bottom of this page.

Messenger

The intelligence passes among cells
like a cruise ship coasting jungle
where happy natives go mysterious ways.
Its passengers loll in deck chairs.
Its ruddy captain twirls his moustache.

Meanwhile, at the most remote,
a renegade parts tall grasses
beside still waters,
barely trusting his knack,
hardly knowing his name.

To and fro currents dandle his skiff.
He dines on fruit and monkey meat,
an arch of boughs comforts him,
he smells he is coming into
a piece of luck.

At the mouth of the river
he remembers commerce
and the thump of engines.
Assuming the port
of a bearer of dispatches,

he threads his sufficient coracle
along the muttering flood
to where dim bulwarks open
with a sigh
and is received.

Memorial Day at the Robert Frost Memorial Picnic Ground in Ripton, Vermont
(for Becky, Lee, Rachael, Robin, Sara A. & Pam)

I sit at a brown table under tall red pines
and wait for the students to come so we can visit
Robert Frost's summer cottage,
tactfully hidden from tourists up an unmarked
road.

A large family (two, three cars) is having
a meal at the far end of the picnic ground.
Their kids ran slalom around tree trunks,
but now are standing by the grill, eating hot dogs
and potato salad with the grown ups.

There is some traffic going by today;
enough motorcycles to salt the silence,
blackflies to pepper the peace.

Every now and then a car pulls in
and a person gets out, or two, three,
strolling under the dark pines
and on where the picnic ground
fades into a blur of young maple.

They glance at the plastic information board,
but let it be because they've stopped by
not to take Frost poems, but bring them.

Is there a T. S. Eliot picnic ground in London,
an A. S. Pushkin picnic ground in Moscow,
even a Henry Miller picnic ground in Big Sur?

Just up the road at Breadloaf Summer School
a caution sign beside the road
warns, "Drive Slowly, Drunken Poets Crossing!"
And such is life, but if it weren't
he'd know to stir things up.

Finish Me

"Finish me." "Finish me," the voices cry
Little voices that follow along behind.
And if I turn and pick them up,
Apply the varnish, set them on the shelf,

No matter how many coats, they're not quite right.
"Finish me!" "Finish me," the tiny voices behind my back
And perhaps they will not end.
The long line of them I see when I turn to the shelf

Is like the beat-up old canoe
My father varnished every spring.
Now it weighs ton,
Old crazed, wacky paint shows through.

"Finish me." "Finish me," the voices cry.
Perhaps I need to visit young Tom, who lives in a house
At the end of the road.

He drinks Moxie from old bottles,
Old canoes breathe damp air under the roof of his shed
The two of us will drink Moxie and tell dreams
About the rivers that have no end

He'll show me how to strip them down
Steam the bent ribs, recover and
Spread the pebbly primer, the smooth
Glossy coats of rich varnish that need the delicate polish.

9

❧ The enclosed dog tag

January 2005

Dear Ali,

————————————————Martin Luther King Day. I'm not sure
of the first word here. Should it be "Happy," "Sad," "Angry,"
"Thoughtful." If I were Secretary of Grammar and Salutations
in the Bush Administration, I guess I'd proclaim it "Thoughtful," though that may not be a word in the lexicon of the
current administration. How about "Have a sly Martin Luther
King Day." THAT's one they'd understand. As I have listened
to the opening barrages of their attack on Social Security (hoping to open up the territory of the innocent and easily-conned
to entrepreneurs, sly-boots, and those who prey on the un-
knowing), I have been getting angrier and angrier. The upshot
is the letter below, which I sent off to the local paper which may
or may not publish it.

Letter to the Editor of the *Monadnock Ledger*

"Looks pretty, talks tough, acts stupid." Is this an unfair
description of the person whose inauguration the country
now celebrates? Yes, it is unfair. Nevertheless we should
look at the record. When George Bush came into office
the country was on a sound fiscal basis thanks to the cooperative work of Republicans in congress and President
Clinton. Big Bush tax reductions for the wealthy disguised by small tax reductions for all took care of that
in short order. When the President was called on this,
a great cry of "Class warfare!" went up from those who
speak for him. The cry was quickly dropped lest the state-
ment be examined carefully.

The grab for Iraqi oil, which is such a failure and

waste of our national treasure, was disguised as an attack on Saddam Hussein and justified as a response to 9/11. Let the administration publish the minutes of the Vice President's "Energy Summit," which took place before 9/11, and it will be made clear what the administration was really up to. It's an interesting fact that the British made a similar grab for Iraqi oil at the end of World War I. Who was it who had the guts to withdraw? Winston Churchill placed common sense above ideology when he realized that the cost of occupation in lives and money far outweighed the profits for British Petroleum Company.

Social Security, closer to home, is to be the next big grab. One can imagine that it will be handled even more clumsily than the occupation of Iraq, although "efficiency" is the administration's watchword. There's more. How did snake oil salesmen advertise their wares in the old days? "I do not come to take your hard earned money, but to do you good." Who do you think will be done good when Wall Street is involved—and how well will they be done—raw, medium or burnt to a crisp? Think carefully about it. Think about the actions of the Halliburton Company in Iraq, and imagine private companies managing your money in similar fashion. Do you want to rush into this in the wake of an administration which rushed into Iraq (and still has not dealt with Bin Laden)? Does the record of this administration so far make you confident that you will be well served by the changes they propose?

"Looks pretty, talks tough, acts stupid." How could we say something so unfair?

Walter Clark

I forgot to say that the immediate stimulus for this note was the enclosed dog tag, a souvenir of my army life. T54 was the year I was drafted. AB is my blood type. The number below my name was my Army serial number, which I was required to memorize. I assume the C in lower left-hand corner was first initial of my last name in case a bullet should do something to the rest of it. The little notch, we were told, is for jamming the tag between the teeth of a battlefield corpse for the greater convenience of graves registration.

March 2005

Lajas, PR

Here are what might be called some items from my journal written during our recent trip. The place is Puerto Rico. We're visiting friends who have a small house in the foothills of the mountains in the southwest corner of the Island, about halfway between St. German and the coast.

> 2 February I'm sitting in the shade of a gnarled tree called a sea-grape. Although it has no grapes, patches of sun filter through its thick, broad, red-veined leaves, providing shade and comfort. Twenty-five feet in front of me wavelets of the Caribbean Seas are lapping on immaculate white sands so fine that the first five feet of ocean are floury white like water coming out at the bottom of a glacier. Just a tad further out the creamy surf turns cloudy green. For the next quarter mile we have turquoise. Then comes the deep ocean blue. There are promontories left and right—not too far away—and there the big waves snap and bark, but here we are lulled by the steady muttered conversation (it could be in Spanish) of small waves. From end to end the beach stretches for a beautiful half mile.

> 3 February So now it is late dawn, a bit before sunrise, yellow and soft clouds to the east. The house itself sits on a small plot of water land in the midst of sunburnt fields pasturing many cows and paved with dry cow-flaps. When I asked whether it was lawful to grill a steak from a cow over

its own flap, I was sent to sit in the corner.

The plain farther out in front of me has room for larger birds. White cattle egrets move from right to left in groups of 3-8, probably chatting as they fly, but too far off to hear. Later, when the sun has burned the mist off, there will be wreathes of somber buzzards circling high up or down low over the house. There's something incongruous about their slow stately motion; as if a Pilgrim Father in broad-brimmed hat were to be seen skateboarding in front of the Meeting House.

Today we may go to the mountains, mountains that rise no more than 4,000 feet, but have grandeur when seen from down here. I must go and get ready.

April 2005

Dear Ali,

Last Friday I drove over to Crotched Mountain where they were having a sugaring off party. It is a combination school and hospital, originally started for kids stricken with polio. It has a nice campus on a hill with view. A couple of big central buildings are flanked by smaller cottages or barracks, where I imagine half a dozen clients have live-in caretakers. I imagine the total number of clients is about 120. Crotched Mountain is a private, non profit foundation and the younger clients, who may make up the majority, are paid for by local school boards throughout the northeast.

Crotched Mountain has its own sugar house, with a two-thousand dollar evaporator inside. The kids tap the trees along with their guides and helpers. I think someone comes in from outside to actually run the evaporator. I had been asked to come to read some poems and also to encourage some of the kids to read their own. There were about forty people at any one time during the half hour of the celebration, of whom a few less than half were in wheelchairs, each with an attendant, although the wheelchairs were motorized for the most part.

After a while an English teacher called all present to order and we gathered in a circle. A student who is eighteen and afflicted with muscular dystrophy introduced me. I was told later that this was a first for him and a big deal. I stood in the middle of the group, revolving slowly and recited Frost's poem, "Into My Own," meanwhile looking for signs in people's eyes that it was coming across. Not too much luck there. Then we broke for a while, after which I read a couple more poems and students were persuaded to read theirs. I didn't think too much of the poems as art, but thought quite a bit of the courage and insight of the writers. After a while—as people broke up and drifted off to other places where they had to be—I had a small dish of ice cream with hot maple syrup on it and headed back here. I have been trying to think of books to send this student, who mentioned that he loves to read.

Not much news from here, except that the weather has broken in spectacular fashion over the weekend, bringing our sugar operation to a halt and washing almost all the ice off the back roof (always a source of concern).

I'm a little past half way with the income tax and feeling a bit like Laocoon in the sculpture, but it will all get done in time, after which I'll be thinking about my annual trip to NELP as well as the usual garden things.

June 2005

Two good bird items. A pair of, or perhaps four, wood thrushes have made our area theirs, so we are treated to lovely singing early and late, as well as on wet days of which we have had not a few. The other good news is of loons. There is a pair visible most days on the pond, and we think they are the same ones who spent last summer here. They do not seem to be nesting, though one can't be sure. According to the book, young mature loons may not breed for several years. As always with loons there are many mysteries.

Here's a bit of haiku that came with the weather:

New beech leaves dangle
in drenching rain. Somebody's
forgotten laundry.

I'm off to dig up the garden—assisted by blackflies and mosquitoes—before it starts to rain again.

Room C 2J, V.A. Hospital

Short Timer

Whooee
I'm getting short, pals
going back to the big E,
Calendar blacked out
as far back as I can see
eyes open;
First sergeant has me
off the duty list,
Company clerk
shuffling his papers,
I'm shuffling my feet,
getting short,
going home.

Headquarters cutting short.
Motor pool take my jeep.
Supply can have my cup
canteen, rifle, clip
I'm getting short
shorter than a toad in heat
I'll never stand in line again.

[*handwritten*]

We were just sticks,
dead wood that trees
let go in the night,
Some they picked up,
Some set by the path
Or in crevices
By the mouths of caves.

We remembered our trees,
Branches dancing the wind,
Our nephews the leaves
Paddling the sun.

How strange were the hands
Of those groundlings.

Things I'm not proud of are many.
When one enters my mind I call *more*.
Come, old fellows, enter my mind
Wearing your black weed
Gather round. Let us listen together
As you raise your lugubrious chant
In which I discern some consonance.

[*handwritten*]

Let me go north to my imagined land,
Yes, north in September to the pond
Where loons howl all night
And the pulled flap shows
Smoke in the morning
Thicker than steam on the water
Where the sound of applause is wing tips
Quick, quick, further, gone

Let me go north further than this,
Past Moosehead, St. Laurence,
To the high table land
Where I will release my canoe
To meet salmon coming to spawn
Where every stream ends in a pond
Like the last one. I will
See bear, and beaver and
Young fisher cats mauling each other

Let me go north to my imagined land
And point the bow downstream,
Making comfortable camps.
I will stop to lie in the sun at noon,
Where Indians camp under blue tarps.
Eagles are there, and ravens,
Where the waters gather and plow
Heavy over the gravel bars.

[*handwritten*]

[Appalachian Trail journal entry] Vermont. Little Rock Shelter

22 September. Today persuaded me that day-hiking is for me from now on and the A.T. can keep its own counsel. It was a beautiful day. I started out a little before 8 and got here at 4 on the dot, but so bushed that it did not seem worth the effort. Trail was not impossible: 45 degrees up, 45 degrees down; 10 horizontal miles and about 2000 feet of elevation. Plenty of people on the trail.

About 2 pm I met a young man who was headed for Maria Hinckley Shelter, where I spent last night. I said I thought it was a long haul—he said it was no problem, 7-8 miles. I did the math just now and realize I have been going about 1 ¼ miles an hour. He would have to do 2-plus to get there before dark. It may not seem like a high rate of speed, but to me it is impossible.

10

❧ How much of hunting consists of being there

June 2006

Dear Ali,
Yesterday was rainy (enough already), but this morning is glorious—cool, windy and with plenty of sun. I'm going to plant parsley after I take this up to the mail box and then do the carpentry work (I hope) for another raised bed of asparagus. I hope that we do not discover, after all is said and done, that we have lost our taste for that vegetable, as there will be acres of it in the back yard, straining away under a blanket of cow manure.

The other day I heard on WGBH an interview with a doctor who is himself a quadriplegic, and whose grandson is autistic. The interviewer asked him how he felt about these afflictions and he said, "Everyone has issues. The thing is to enjoy the good things and to make use of the talents you have." She asked him what he would say to his grandson, and his answer was something along the lines of "Know that you are loved and be sure that things will work out for you." I thought those were good words.

January 2007

Dear Ali,
"So how do you keep busy, now that you're retired?" "Incompetence, the great busifier!"

In this spirit, I have to say that your marvelous Christmas present [microwave oven] is still in its box. As a matter of policy I have not asked your Mom where she would like it, but I have picked my spot and intend for it to suddenly appear in place— along with a bag of special zapper popcorn. That should fetch her.

Around 7 a.m. I fell into the white rocker with a jar of coffee in my trembling hand—JUST in time to catch a glimpse of a young otter who was briefly visible along the shelf of new ice that had formed along the inner rocks. I watched carefully for ten minutes, but did not catch sight of him again. It made me realize how much of hunting consists of being there and being ready.

June 2007

I woke at 4:24 this morning and looked at my watch. Ordinarily that is not a good time to wake, as the mind tends to rev up just when you want it to lie down for another couple of hours. But this morning I had the chance for some nature observation without throwing off the covers. It turns out that birds, led by the robins, have a big party or confabulation at this hour. It is quite like the kind of cocktail party one imagines taking place out in Hollywood—where everyone is a star. Nobody seems to listen to anyone else and all are going at the top of their lungs. What is it all about? This is MY space? Thank you God? Yeah! We're putting the whole thing together once again? Who knows? The amazing thing is that it all ceases quite abruptly in about half an hour's time and everybody drives off to work. My mind was so shocked that it lay down as ordered and went back to sleep.

Sitting with my breakfast coffee just now and enjoying, as always, our lovely pond, I noticed that the fish were rising. Perhaps they do this every morning (imitating the birds?), but because the pond was perfectly still I could see that often they were not coming up just to snap up a bug. Some were actually on the surface, or just below it as if engaged in philosophical investigations; "What is this world beyond our ken?" Just then an enormous bird flew across my line of sight. At first I thought it was the heron of the day. I had just time to realize that it was not, but instead a great bald eagle before it disappeared. I didn't have time to see whether it had anything in its grasp, but recall that bald eagles are fish eaters, and that I had once watched one on Chesuncook in Maine swooping down to pick fish out of the far waters. I think my friend here was dining on the laziest of philosophers.

The loons have been gone for over a month—probably to Nuba-nusit or some bigger lake where they can compare notes. I think it unlikely that they or any other loons will raise a brood here, as getting off the water is a bit of a trick for them. They circle the pond twice before they can get above tree level. I think it would be even harder for chicks. I was surprised, then, to see a loon coming down the pond in my direction. Its breast seemed quite white, and I noticed a certain unloonlike nervousness of move-ment. It wasn't a loon, but a diver of some sort, smaller and less predictable. Looked for it just now in the book and the nearest I could get was "Bufflehead," which seemed unlikely and makes me a Bafflehead. Out of the corner of my eye I saw enormous wings overhead. Lost sight of the little bird, but then it popped up close to shore, seemingly having managed a feat of matter transmission. The coffee, meanwhile, was beginning to take ef-fect, so that when the big wings appeared again I was ready to at-tach them, to a more or less reliable degree, to a bald eagle. The B? bird seemed unconcerned, or perhaps he felt he had baffled the eagle with his matter-transmitting tactics, and so moved out fairly rapidly a couple of hundred yards offshore where, to me, he seemed like fast food. There he loitered rapidly in where-did-I-leave-it fashion for five minutes or so, then picked up his wings and flew off, soon disappearing because of his size. The eagle never appeared again, although I was ready for it. The moral, I think, is like the morals of so many of those nature stories that (unlike this one) never get written. The moral is that nature stories don't have morals, despite the activities of such as Ernest Thomson Seton, whose book *Wild Animals I Have Known* was parodied by a reviewer as "Wild Animals I Alone Have Known".

Early yesterday morning I saw swirlies on the surface of the pond; the kind that large fish make when they are rounding up small fry. But it was much too late in the year for this sort of activity. I imagine all the large fish as lying around on the bottom of the pond muttering advice to the frogs who are dug in below them. As I watched the patches of boil they resolved themselves into small heads, sticking above the water and moving rather fast. "Beavers on speed?" I wondered. No! It was otters, a family of three, I think, though they moved so fast in the water it was hard to be sure at first. Eventually one climbed out on the rock in front of the house. It held a fish about eight inches long between its front paws, and meditatively nibbled away—reminding me of a small child with a large popsicle. After it finished another otter climbed up and repeated the process. Then I saw a smaller one on the ice that edged the pond, not looking very dapper. The eating continued for quite a while. After all the large torpid fish had been disposed of the three of them swam off toward the neighbors' house next door. It was quite a display, and not likely to be repeated for some time as, lo and behold, the pond is frozen this morning, a complete job accomplished in one night with the help of falling snow and twenty degree weather. I had had ample warning and was able to complete one of my wood piles with the help of the log splitter your mother gave me. By the time I finished it was too dark to haul it back down here, so it's up there, along with an enormous pile of logs, awaiting my further attention.

It is impossible to hype
The subtle flavor of rock tripe.

[*handwritten*]

Belly Says

I am the Middle Man.

Whatever comes to me
I make meal,
Building rafter and bone.

I am the thumping stone
That chafes the lower one,

One eye on the hopper,
The other on the sack.

I crack at dawn and dusk
Like frozen lake.

Without this gut
You front no daunting task.

Death by Custard

A phone solicitation tonight
By a voice from Death with Dignity.

By all means, but let it be pleasant
I would go gently into that good night.

And if I get to choose
It's death by custard where I take my stand

In frank nostalgia for the days
I turned the crank below the kitchen porch.

First off with wheelbarrow to the
ice-house, as chilly as a church

Digging the winter skin of lake
out of its sawdust casement.

The cake once washed must be
chipped with the old ice pick

Only —— for this special gel.

Then god appears with her sweet smelling bowl
of thick vanilla'd cream.

And in one hand a canvas
bag of salt, rough pebbled
· · · · · · · · · · · ·

Yes, death by custard
Is the road I'd choose

The long, roped arteries and veins
That lead to somewhere

Slowly pilling up with fat
A surfeit/

As for Prayer

As for prayer—
even without dogma
sometimes you just have to praise
and thank and say "yea"
like a little boy in the back yard
firing caps at the blue, blue sky—
at whatever it is has nothing for us
but two eyes and a short span;

and you can imagine
one of those harsh young men,
a true cowboy, on a summery morn,
full of coffee and beans,
having just had a good dump
behind a tussock,
the horse fresh under him,
first smoke of the day
between his fingers;
and catching that glint of light
on the horizon—
he hears himself
say "Railhead! Railhead!"
the winged words lifting away.

Because you can imagine all that
and know how hard to saddle a horse,
you will keep on lifting—
laboriously filling your bucket
at the bottom of the hole;
thinking to see the dawn star
at noon, or a face
peering over the well kerb—
Thinking maybe to strike water.

Ice Going out on Lake Wentworth

A noise like gently shaken chandeliers.
Into the cove a south wind chivying
Trash ice is sounding changes on the air,
The minute clangor of again turning.
The mock-carnation lake one disrepair,
The Ice Queen's palace in a drop of snow
Its fierce geometry dissolving here,
Slide quietly before a flower blows,
Poising along this sullen anarchy
From which the quirky blast of green reform
Will snatch an eager cabinet once more,
Turning from politics of chill and warm
For the time being, insubstantial hour
To rest apart from cycles and their power.

October Dawn

October—dawn—

west wind strikes

cloud soldiers off

mountain pond;

they march off

dissolving.

One red maple

sounds alarm

on tawny green hill.

Glorious to see. Glorious!

And why not glorious

Is our undoing!

Finding Your Poem

You can find it with the poetry tool on our website,
follow its careful footsteps to the last stop.

There it is—gigging frogs
from an airboat at four a.m.,
wearing night glasses and feral grin.

Does it have wings?
Will it creep into the folds of your clothing?
Does its hoarse breath knock you awake?

Can it whisper
life into hazel buds,
kick the high can-can

in drabbest fug
of Irish pub, slip weasel
tracks off April snow?

Look for it in packets of old letters,

You can find it with the poetry tool
hanging from the bent nail
in the back of your head

[*On language*]   ✓✓

We are the tree, in which
It roosts on its passage
Somewhere else.

[*handwritten*]

Coming down slope in late autumn afternoon
The sun dancing dappled through the rusty oak.
Pack sweaty and swinging on bag, blanket warmer yet
Air sharp as cider to drink with hint of smoke

One who has been climbing, climbing must now descend
Has hearing of owls, their beckoning calls
Hint of something; then sees the line of a roof
Or is it only a rock

The hut with twist of slow gray rising
Like a scarf flung over the moon
Whose pale half hangs high in dissolving blue

The unlatched door.

[handwritten]

Autumn Rain

Senior, he sits at ease before the glassed-in wall
A cup of morning coffee in his hand.
Night sentry has taught him to (appreciate) a roof.
Rain dimples on the glass and pond
Bemusingly and calls his mind awake
To ask if it is dry between the drops,
To view the blurring silhouette
Of pines across the pond appraisingly.
In the front yard copper beech leaves cling,
The tart oak leaves hang like laundry.
Gray clouds sag like dugs of sheep.
Everything, he thinks, like everything.
His mind, now supple as a fakir's boy,
Climbs up profanity.
"Goddam, it's beautiful—and what a gift."

[*handwritten*]

AFTERWORD

MY FATHER'S CORRESPONDENCE with me was pretty one-sided, alas. Daddy wrote frequently, about once every one or two months. He even wrote me when we both lived in Ann Arbor and were able to see each other in person. I left for Seattle right after college graduation, and spent the next ten years in the northwest. During this time, I only saw my parents once or twice a year and fell out of touch with my extended family. My infrequent letters home were generally restricted to events that I thought were newsworthy. Nevertheless, my father's letters came regularly.

Mostly they reported on the state of life in New Hampshire, and his various doings in retirement. They were full of advice and relevant newspaper clippings; in this way, they were reflective of the letters that his own mother had sent him weekly, when he was in college. I'm pleased that he preserved the tradition that she had taught him. His letters were often hilarious, and his ideas and uses of words were unique. The details of the weather and the countryside were reassuring to me in my minimum-wage, citified existence, and it was cheering to receive drafts of his poetry and journal entries. I was aware that he wrote poetry frequently, and receiving poems in the mail made me feel like a part of his creative process. Every year for St. Patrick's Day he would include a humorous Hallmark card, and the accompanying letter would tell me more about his mother's (Irish) side of the family. In almost every letter, he would include the titles of one or two books that he thought I might like.

Overall, I got the impression that he was very happy in his retirement, and absolutely in love with New Hampshire. My father was always an experimenter and a dilettante, and the combination of free time and access to the wilderness gave him many new things to do. He expanded his hobbies—writing, baking, weaving, logging, gardening, carpentry, cooking, and of course hiking. When I came to visit, I noticed that tools and equipment had begun to accumulate—he had a few new chainsaws and a small workshop. There were bags of fertilizer in the garage, bags of flour in the basement, many piles of split wood, and a collection of camping equipment and hiking boots. Even though he was keeping himself happily busy, he continued to take my life into consideration in his letters to me. They included useful financial advice and reassurances about how to live life as a young adult, and how not to worry about how valuable I might (or might not) be to the wide world. The letters were sustaining when I was lonely and feeling frustrated, and they kept me connected to both of my parents, reminding me that even though it was 3,000 miles away, I did have a home.

Eventually, I moved from Seattle to Boston, to be closer to my parents. Luckily, I was able to see a lot of my father over the last few years of his life.

—ALISON CLARK

BIOGRAPHICAL NOTES

A CLOSER LOOK AT WALTER'S LIFE STORY may help toward understanding the writer. This summary adds to the editors' views that of his brother, Jonathan.

I

Walter Houston Clark, Jr., was born on October 6, 1931, in Pittsfield, Massachusetts, the elder child of two high school English teachers. Prior to her marriage, Ruth O'Brien Clark had taught at a high school in Milwaukee. Five years before his son's birth, Walter Houston Clark had helped to found Lenox School, a small Episcopal preparatory school near Pittsfield designed to educate the sons of ministers unable to afford more prestigious schools. Costs were minimized by having students wait on tables and help with maintenance. Since it housed fewer than forty boys during its first twenty years, Lenox School may have helped to seed Walter junior's vision of an environment where students could learn from each other as well as from their instructors.

The simplicity of the school was paralleled by the family's lifestyle. Jonathan was born five and a half years after Walter. The two children lived with their parents on the Lenox School grounds in a five-room house attached to a dormitory housing about a dozen boys, who were overseen by their father. Socializing was part of the children's world. Reading was a main entertainment in the family. The parents read aloud to each other and both read to each son from an eclectic assortment of children's books, and, ultimately, novels.

By all accounts Walter was precocious, starting first grade at four years old, though for social reasons he was then kept back for a year. A family friend in her nineties remembers Walter as a child of five or six running up to her husband and asking, "Read any good books lately?"

New Hampshire living was important to him in several ways. The Clark family summer place in Wolfeboro, built by his grandfather on Lake Wentworth, brought him social family pleasures and adventures. It also gave him solitude. Years later he could point out the "reading rock," on an island, to which he paddled as a child to read quietly. From age

10 until a year after he finished the army, he demonstrated by returning to it how important YMCA Camp Belknap on Lake Winnipesaukee was for him. From camper to counselor, division leader, sermon-giver, sailing teacher, newspaper founder, and librettist of a camp opera, he attracted a following in summers between 1941 and 1957. A friend has kept samples of his perceptions, here about hurrying to beach sailboats:

> Tonight we had to bring them in again, a scene of great beauty; with great waves, thunder-bearing clouds and a fingernail moon fractured into a thousand pieces along the waters . . .

His formal education brought him challenges. At age 13, in the fall of 1944, he entered Lenox School as a freshman, where his father was serving as headmaster, and was unmercifully scapegoated. He left the school in January and went to live for the remaining school year with his grandmother in New Jersey. During the following six years the family moved frequently due to his father's transition into college teaching, which included the colleges of Bowdoin and Middlebury. After graduating from Middlebury, Vermont, High School, he enrolled for a "year 13" at Phillips Exeter Academy. It was at Exeter, he felt, that he first experienced the power of poetry and of outstanding teaching.

He graduated from Swarthmore College in 1954 with honors and with a prize in poetry. He chose to follow up with a summer in Alaska and two years in the army before enrolling in graduate school at Harvard University. There he received an MA in English, and a Ph.D in philosophy of education in 1965. In the next year he published a book of poetry, *Nineteen Poems* by Walter Clark, comprising the first issue of *Little Square Review*, edited by John Ridland, who was to become his lifelong friend.

Walter taught at the University of Michigan for twenty-eight years, as assistant professor from 1965 and as associate professor after 1970. His courses ranged from freshman composition through seminars in poetry writing, literature, Frost and Thoreau, and graduate courses in critical theory and philosophy of education. He received two teaching awards from University of Michigan and a medal of merit from the University of Graz during a Fulbright lectureship. Along with publications of individual poems and scholarly articles, he published a second book of poetry, *View from Mount Paugus*, in 1976. He had privately depressed periods, as a letter to his friend John Ridland confessed. Perhaps comparable to his feelings about the institution of religion, he felt the weight of a gulf between education and the educational institution.

As his life evolved, excellent innovation in teaching became Walter's major career focus. Probably his proudest contribution in life was the founding and co-directing of the University of Michigan New England Literature Program (NELP), which he led with Alan Howes from 1975 to 1991, and visited from then on. This was and is a field program of 30 to 40 students and teachers writing and studying New England authors in New Hampshire during the University's spring term. All courses are seminars; all maintenance work is cooperative. Students keep daily journals and learn basic outdoor-living and hiking skills. They learn to share and teach literature. Change Magazine was the first to recognize this program with a national teaching award in 1976. Many of the thousand NELP alumnae have written that it was the best learning experience they ever had. The continuation of NELP, at this writing in its 37th year, is a legacy that multiplies. By 2007 Walter had raised an endowment to ensure the future director's position.

His most comprehensive description of NELP is in "The New England Literature Program" in *Teaching Environmental Literature*, ed. Frederick O. Waage (New York, 1985). Later he summed up what he saw as the most significant elements in the program's continuing success:

> Size, environment and relative brevity are all factors that contribute to the unique character of NELP, but it is the attitudes toward students in relation to subject matter that really distinguish it. NELP is, above all, a place where students are taken seriously—in writing, in discussion of the texts they read and in all other aspects of student life.

Walter married Francelia Mason in 1967. She too had a love of New Hampshire land, developed a teaching career at University of Michigan, and in time became a dedicated teacher in the NELP program. Their daughter, Alison, benefited as a child by joining the NELP community each spring, and graduated University of Michigan in 1994. As a family they loved long summers in New Hampshire, and when feasible joined in the active and varied outdoor life that appears in Walter's letters to Alison. In 1993 the couple retired from the University to a home they had built on Francelia's inherited land in the Monadnock region. From there came the 49 poems and the fifteen years of letters viewing a new and cherished life. In May 2008 Walter died suddenly of a heart attack, during a Sunday afternoon walk, in his woodlot beside the cords of wood he had split and stacked for the winter.

Was I surprised!
Uncle Death stepped out of the wood
All of a sudden
Like Rip Van Winkle
Smelling of
Leaves and mud.
He had the family eyes.
"Give over ploughing," he said.
"It's been a long time,"
Slitting a straw,
"Are there children?" he said.
"Two boys and a girl.
Will you be long?"
"Only tonight.
Gone by tomorrow."
"I'll tell Mary
To make up the bed."
"No need," he said. ` — Walter Clark, *Nineteen Poems*, 1966

II

Many of my brother's later poems in this volume refer to death and topics concerning faith and prayer. Reading these and discussing them with Francelia and Alison I realized that our parents' spiritual lives and interest in metaphysics played an important role in initiating Walter's interest in these matters.

Our parents' courtship of three years was marked by debate about the religious education of their children. As a Roman Catholic, Mother felt bound by her church's edict that any children must be raised as Catholic. As a Presbyterian, Daddy argued that such a stipulation would restrict his influence on their religious upbringing. Seeming to resolve the issue, neither parent realized that as a married couple after 1930 they would face twenty years of friction over it. On Sunday morning we attended Mass with Mother. Upon our return home, Daddy required us to have a "Sunday School Lesson"—readings from the Old and New Testament of the Bible and memorization of verses—before we were released to enjoy the day. The matter resolved itself in 1958, when Daddy authored a widely acclaimed textbook on the psychology of religion. The book brought him into contact with Catholic scholars in Europe and America and moderated his view of Catholic educational institutions.

For the two of us, rather than making matters of faith and religious practice so politicized that they became forbidden areas of exploration, the struggle deepened our awareness of choices. Both parents, while holding to tenets each felt indispensable to our religious upbringing, entertained a larger view of spiritual practice. Indeed, they were probably attracted to each other because their spiritual aspirations transcended the doctrines of their religious faiths. Perhaps because of this, each parent responded to passages in literature concerning spiritual growth—Daddy tracing the evolution of the biblical God between Old and New Testament, Mother reading to us from "The Chambered Nautilus" the conclusion beginning "Build thee more stately mansions, O my soul."

Both of us ceased to practice as Catholics in our twenties, a source of deep disappointment to Mother. I believe we felt confined by formal religion's theological and moral maps. Yet neither parent had shrunk from exposing us to the myopia of formal religion. A Benedictine monk, at a school where my brother had spent a summer during high school, put it most succinctly for me, with a smile: "In the Beginning, God created Man and ever since, Man has been returning the compliment!"

When I read Walter's poem, "Isn't: Two Routes to the Same Hut," I wondered whether he might have had our parents' struggles in mind. I felt that he had regarded the stop signs posted at the edge of the religious reservation as invitations to press onward into more rugged, less charted territories.

III

My brother was a welcoming person. He received me into the family with delight. One of my earliest memories is of him encouraging me to give a speech. I recall standing up and uttering some garbled words to which he responded with enthusiastic applause. Later he created games and projects tailored to my level of interest.

The contrast between his enjoyment of people and his thirst for solitude helps me appreciate the person he was. In his maturity, while he loved the gatherings of the Clark extended family at Wolfeboro, and cared a great deal about our land and its use by future generations, Walter also built a tiny shack in the woods, reminiscent of Thoreau's hut. When he couldn't be found around the house, chances were he had retreated to his shack where he could escape the summer buzz.

In the days after Walter's death a host of memories arose. In one, I was six years old. He and I were in the back seat of Granny's convertible. The top was down as we traveled through the White Mountains. When I looked behind us I was suddenly aware that the mountain we had passed seemed to rise up rather than sink lower on the landscape, an optical illusion created by the rapidly receding trees lining each side of the road. Now, in mourning, it expressed a truth. As the recollections of my lifetime brotherhood with Walter flashed by, he who had begun an endless journey into the past rose up like a mountain, a giant in my life.

JONATHAN CLARK
July 2011

NOTES ON THE TEXTS

BOTH WALTER'S LETTERS AND POEMS from retirement are selected for this publication. Alison has selected the most vivid place-related and self-related writing from his letters to her across these years, totaling some eighty pages. Francelia has selected from his retirement computer files and handwritten pages all of the poems about either New Hampshire or self that registered distinct and complete in message—which is nearly all of them. She is aware that Walter left any blank space or parenthetical alternate choice of phrase as signifying "unfinished." (Notably, as a teaching exercise, he used to remove a word from any author's poem, leaving a space, and ask the students to create their best choice.) Francelia also knows from Walter's publication files and his lifetime collaboration with friend and poet John Ridland, at University of California in Santa Barbara, that he continued to be strongly interested in publishing. John has pointed out that Walter did not necessarily finish a poem with the change he had considered adding.

All poems are chronological, as far as can be dated, or if undated then guessed by internal evidence within their designated span of years. An exception is that poetry viewing the natural world is placed first in each collection. All selections from letters are chronological but for a couple of condensed subjects, such as learning carpentry and teaching Thoreau, and the separation of two especially vivid entries—"Toads on the Trail" and "New Year's Eve in Nelson." When a letter to Alison contains a poem, there is where the poem appears, regardless of its date in the computer file.

As for mechanics, all of Walter's handwritten poems carry the note "[handwritten]" at bottom of the page. The Contents pages carry the first line of poems untitled in the text. A diagonal slash at the end of a line that appears to end a poem is the editorial mark based on evidence within the text that "more may follow." Throughout the text, all parentheses are Walter's; all square brackets mark editorial additions.

Following are notes on specific texts, keyed by the page numbers on which they appear.

p. v "Moonlit May Night (Eichendorff variant)." Walter's perhaps best-loved poem was composed for the manuscript Cells, 1986, intended for publication. His love of language extended well beyond his own. He had discovered German poetry with a Swarthmore College teacher he valued, lived for a time in Germany, and took a teaching Fulbright in Austria. He read and worked with poetry of Rilke and developed a library of Bach's music.

Walter's variant seems to introduce his own values as a poet as well as his intense sense of place. Below, for comparison, is the poem "Mondnacht," by Joseph von Eichendorff (1788–1857), from *Geistliche Gedichte*, reprinted in *Gedichte eine Auswahl*, 1968). Following the original, "Mondnacht" is translated by kindness of Walter's friend Steve Schuch.

Mondnacht

Es war, als hätt' der Himmel
Die Erde still geküßt,
Daß sie im Blütenschimmer
Von ihm nun träumen müßt'.

Die Luft ging durch die Felder,
Die Ähren wogten sacht,
Es rauschten leis die Wälder,
So sternklar war die Nacht.

Und meine Seele spannte
Weit ihre Flügel aus,
Flog durch die stillen Lande,
Als flöge sie nach Haus.

Moon Night (free verse English translation by Steve Schuch*)

It was as if Sky had kissed the Earth,
So quietly that as she shimmered in her blossoms,
Her dreams must be of him.

The breeze moved through the fields
Of gently nodding grain,
Rustling softly in the woods,
So star-clear was the night.

And my soul spread wide its wings,
Flying through the quiet lands,
As if it were flying home.

* Eichendorff was a lyric poet in the lineage of Goethe and Heine. This well-known poem was set to music by both Schumann and Brahms. In the original German, the word "Himmel" means both heaven and sky. Walter's subsequent poem used the word "sky," and so I used that in the opening line of this translation.—S.S.

p. 5 "Down the Great Meadow" . . . Walter enclosed the entry from a journal. The editors, to begin the flow of letters, have styled this entry as a letter.

p. 6 "March on Figured Ground" first appeared in Cells.

p. 7 "Gerard (draft 4)." The four drafts are numbered in Walter's computer file.

p. 8 "Splitting Oak" was included in a letter to John Ridland after the summer's clearing to build in 1983, and Walter presented it in reading a "calendar" of poetry in Wolfeboro.

p. 9 "Walking Up the Hill" is a sample of Walter's typed revision, showing typed alternatives and the typed note "moonlight not colors."

p. 20 "Hylidae" and "Haiku." "Ecstatic assent" is almost strong enough to typify NELP students' response to spring peepers. Both these poems may have come from a NELP field trip to Lake Wentworth. There, Walter's screened "shack" was his spot closest to nature for both hearing and watching.

p. 21 "Martian Anthropologists" was conceived in Ann Arbor and considerably revised.

p. 23 [A NELP writing.] "My Vantage Point" was a favorite assignment for spontaneous student writing. A favorite teaching device was to join in the writing.

p. 28 "The Barbecue of the Virtues." Walter enjoyed the idea of "roasting" as an honor, which he did aloud with this poem. His friend and colleague Parker Huber is a Thoreau scholar extraordinaire, who prefers to validate Thoreau's experienced truths by experiencing them himself, by walking, for example, from Peterborough across Monadnock's summit to Troy Depot, seventeen miles in ten and one half hours. ("Following Thoreau," in *Where the Mountain Stands Alone*, ed. Howard Mansfield, University Press of New England, Hanover, 2006)

p. 32 "Fifty Springs Are Little Room." The title refers to this line in A. E. Housman's "Loveliest of Trees, the Cherry Now." Housman's poem seems in part to jest with the boundaries of aging and springtime. The analogy suggests that Walter's poem need not have been revised from earlier, as its placement here indicates, but was composed at Hunt's Pond in the undated file where it was found. This one conveys beauty, not resignation.

p. 33 [Journal entries from Canoeing Maine.] A two-week, single-canoe journey from Greenville, Maine, across Moosehead Lake, down the Penobscot and Allagash to a spot fifteen miles down the St. John River, by Walter and NELP teacher and former student Sam Manhart, fostered journals by both of them. The ranger who flew them back out commented, "Nobody does this." A condensed form of their combined journal is in *Rivendell*, ed. Sebastian Matthews, I: 2 (*North of Boston*, Summer 2003), 207-230.

p. 55 "In Praise of English," revised over time, originally appeared in the festschrift *A Garland for Harry Duncan*. A revised version is in *Solo: A Journal of Poetry*, (Solo Press, vol. 5, 2002).

p. 58 "Gerard Manley Hopkins." This letter to Alison contained the version shown earlier, "Gerard (draft 4)." Soon, however, Walter had written this, his final version, and under the principle that if sent to Alison, there is where it appears, we have placed the final version here.

p. 60 "Umbazooksus." Originally part of Cells, it honors Umbazooksus Lake, the most remote lake on an Allagash trip, leading obliquely to the Mud Pond Carry, where one portages the canoe in a running brook bed and where even Thoreau got lost. It was Walter's favorite part of those trips.

p. 61 "There are no dead letters" is the first and possibly most spontaneous of the handwritten poems. John Ridland and Jonathan Clark have helped to decipher handwriting in these poems. Here alone, a phrase [of wine] is bracketed because we readers could not be sure of the words.

p. 63 "Words to the Same End." In fact House of Mercy Hospital, in Pittsfield, Massachusetts, is where both Walter and Jonathan were born.

p. 67 "Since it is March we are sugaring." The description, slightly revised, is published as "Sugaring Time," in turn acknowledging *The Monadnock Ledger*, in *Views and Voices: Hancock, NH*, ed. Margaret Carlson and Marcia Amidon Lusted (Hancock, NH., 2006), pp. 41-42.

p. 69 "Toads on the Trail." The journal entry, originally dated August 2001, was sent to Alison in 2003, and moved here for sake of balance.

p. 72 "Gluck (On a line from Anthony Hecht)" was revised, apparently from two poems, themselves revised, in Ann Arbor. The volume in Walter's library is *The Venetian Vespers: Poems by Anthony Hecht* (New York: Atheneum, 1979). The line that strikes the editors in context is in "A Cape Cod Lullabye." The conception of "more light," known as Goethe's last words, drew Walter's ongoing attention.

p. 76 "Tryptich." In addition to "F, H, C," the several drafts of this poem bore the alternate titles "Notes for an Orchestral Suite," and "Memo to St. Paul." The subtitle "(for emily)" may refer only to the poem indicated as "hope."

p. 89 "Last night we went to Nelson." This scene has been moved here from January 1, 2001, for sake of balance.

p. 93 "Off now to read Walt Whitman's Song of Myself." Walter refers to preparing for his first reading for the community with the readers who became an important pleasure of his life.

p. 96 "Puzzled Dust" was published in *Rivendell*, I: 2, 48.

p. 104 "First Run" was published in *Views and Voices*, p. 43. The gift that inspired him was from friends Ron and Kathy Notkin, drawn from the maples of Enosburg Falls, Vermont. Some of the drafts carry the subtitle "Homage to R. F."

p. 111 "They Were Traveling." The earliest version is in a poetry exchange with John Ridland in 1990, and was revised in many versions in New Hampshire.

p. 112 "The Prince" began in Ann Arbor, the one from three on related themes that he chose for revision in New Hampshire.

p. 114 "Messenger" has an earlier form in an exchange with John Ridland in 1981.

p. 115 "Memorial Day." The dedication is to Rachael Cohen, NELP teacher, and five students on a field trip they were sharing into Frost country.

p. 117 "Finish me." As mentioned above, this poem is the only reference to the handwritten pile of them that was growing on the open shelf. Walter was working at length to repair the old canoe with Tom Seavey, antique-canoe restorer.

p. 121 "Lajas, PR" The two excerpts are parts of longer journal entries which were published in *The Occasional Moose* (May 2005), the literary magazine edited by Jane Eklund within the *Monadnock Ledger*.

p. 128 "Let Me Go North." The details are imagined but also summoned, not only from outstanding canoeing experiences on the Allagash, but much earlier on the waters East of Wawa, Ontario, and, especially in the last ten lines, on the Macmillan and Pelly rivers in Yukon Territory.

p. 140 "Ice Going Out on Lake Wentworth" was being revised from its appearance in Walter Clark, *View from Mount Paugus and Other Poems,* (Omaha: University of Nebraska, 1976) ; 2d ed. (Ann Arbor, MI: Bee Line Press, 1979). It appears that Walter was removing the presence of a person who turns away from this scene, so that the entire sonnet would belong to the lake.

p. 151 "Uncle Death," in Walter Clark, *Nineteen Poems*, comprising volume I of *The Little Square Review*, ed. John Ridland (Santa Barbara, CA, 1966). *Nineteen Poems* was Walter's first book of poetry.

1.

Crinkling my sleep ear,
The chill of spring peepers
And underneath those
Blabber of toads.

When was my first year
To hear and partake of
This wafer of known?
When my last one?